THE SONG FOREVER NEW

Lent and Easter
with Charles Wesley

Paul Wesley Chilcote

Morehouse Publishing
NEW YORK · HARRISBURG · DENVER

Unless otherwise noted, the Scripture quotations contained herein are from the New Revised Standard Version Bible, copyright © 1989 by the Division of Christian Education of the National Council of Churches of Christ in the U.S.A. Used by permission. All rights reserved.

The suggestions are drawn from *The Hymnal 1982*, the authorized hymnal of the Episcopal Church; but the hymn tunes and meters can be located in the index of the standard hymnals of many traditions.

Morehouse Publishing, 4775 Linglestown Road, Harrisburg, PA 17112

Morehouse Publishing, 445 Fifth Avenue, New York, NY 10016

Morehouse Publishing is an imprint of Church Publishing Incorporated.

ISBN-13: 978-0-8192-2373-9 (paperback)

Cover design by Jennifer Glosser

Library of Congress Cataloging-in-Publication Data

A catalog record for this book is available from the Library of Congress.

Printed in the United States of America

09 10 11 12 13 14   10 9 8 7 6 5 4 3 2 1

For
Dick and Lorena Campbell,
Lamar Runestad,
L. L. Fleming,
and Rodney Wynkoop,
choir directors who have helped me sing
The Song Forever New

CONTENTS

PART THREE: FORMATS FOR MORNING AND EVENING PRAYER

INTRODUCTION

Praise the Lord, you blessed ones,
   Praise your glorious Lord and ours,
Principalities, and thrones,
   Join with all the heavenly powers;
Angels, that in strength excel,
   Here your utmost strength employ,
Let your ravished spirits swell
   Filled with endless praise and joy . . .
   In the song forever new.

Lent and Easter prepare us to join this chorus. The song that is forever new for us proclaims the mystery and glory of God's redeeming love. Like God's grace, it is new every morning. We have come to know it in the death and resurrection of Jesus Christ. This song shapes our lives and unites us in mission. The purpose of this little devotional work is two-fold. First, I hope that these scripture readings, hymns, meditations, and prayers will help you to reflect with greater intentionality about the meaning of redemption. What does it mean to have the name of Christ "written upon your heart," that "new, best name of Love?" Second, I seek to locate Wesley squarely in his Anglican heritage and to enable many outside (and within) the circle of Methodism to discover him as a profound mentor for faithful Christian discipleship. With regard to this second goal—and to set the larger context for these readings—permit me to say just a few things about the spirituality of this great man of God and his appreciation for the seasons of preparation and celebration into which we enter during Lent and Easter.

Charles Wesley's vision of the Christian life revolved around clear principles that have stood the test of time and resonate fully with his Anglican heritage. His understanding of redemption in Christ—what has been called the Wesleyan "way of salvation"—revolved around three dynamic movements of God related primarily to the human heart or spirit: repentance, faith, and holiness. With his older brother, John, he sometimes described repentance as the porch of religion, faith as the door, and holiness as religion itself. Reflecting a viewpoint unique in his day and our own, he defined *repentance* as a true self-understanding. He drew this language, most certainly, from the experience of the prodigal son who "came to himself" in the realization that he had strayed so far from his true home (Luke 15). While repentance involves remorse and contrition, it carries a strong relational connotation for Wesley, the initial turning of the heart and life homeward to God.

Faith is the gift of trust in those things we cannot see, especially "Christ's love for me." But the word "faith" often functions as a shorthand symbol for the more specific concept of "justification by grace through faith," which refers to the experience of having been accepted and pardoned by God through faith in Jesus Christ. Some Christians would simply describe this as conversion, but with regard to this dynamic movement of God in the human heart, Wesley emphasizes the grace-enabled ability to entrust our lives to God. Wesley was careful not to separate faith in Christ from growth in grace. *Holiness* is another shorthand term that refers to the whole process of becoming like Christ once we have experienced God's unconditional love. It includes the idea of sanctification, the process of growing in grace and love, and Christian perfection—perhaps the most important of all Wesleyan concepts—which refers to the love of God and neighbor filling one's heart and life.

The phrase *grace upon grace*, then, aptly summarizes Wesley's understanding of the Christian life. Discipleship begins in grace, grows in grace, and finds its ultimate completion in God's grace. Grace is God's unmerited love, restoring our relationship to God and renewing God's own image in our lives. Life, to put it rather simply, is all about a God who delights in relationships that liberate and restore the human spirit, that enable us to love in the same way we have been loved by Christ. Drinking deeply from the wells of his Anglican heritage, Wesley developed this *comprehensive* vision of theology and the Christian life characterized by an unusually wide embrace. In his vision of "redeemed life," he carefully balanced personal salvation and social justice, faith and works, heart and head, Word and Sacrament. Immersion in the means of grace—both acts of piety and acts of mercy—fueled the Wesleyan movement within Anglicanism and enabled it to become a powerful evangelical and Eucharistic awakening.

Charles Wesley left behind his most important legacy in an amazing collection of hymns—his gift of song to the church. He believed that singing praise to God transforms the singer. Sacred song shapes the people of God. His lyrical theology points to the centrality of grace, encourages accountable discipleship in such a way as to promote holiness of heart and life, and proclaims the ultimate foundation of all things in God's unconditional love for us all in Christ Jesus. The Wesleyan hymns help us rediscover our essential identity as children of God. They teach us how to integrate Christian faith and practice. They enable us to experience the inclusivity of the community of faith through the very act of singing together. Wesley's hymns continue to function as a powerful tool in God's work of spiritual transformation and renewal.

In his lyrical theology, both the redemptive work of Christ and the restoration of God's image in the believer figure prominently. Sacred texts from Wesley's *Hymns for those that seek, and those that have Redemption in the Blood of Jesus Christ* (1747) and *Hymns for Our Lord's Resurrection* (1746) are particularly suited to the themes of Lent and Easter. The hymns of the former collection are a lyrical expression of the Wesleyan theology of salvation, which sought to recapture the grace-oriented vision of the *Book of Common Prayer* and the *Homilies* of the Church of England. The latter collection not only celebrates the Resurrection of Jesus, but emphasizes the newness of life available to all people in Christ, turning life into a song of praise and gratitude to God. Selections from both of Wesley's collections are featured in the volume, including *Come, Sinners, to the Gospel Feast* and *Love Divine,*

All Loves Excelling, as well as hymns such as "And Can It Be," "Christ the Lord Is Risen Today" and "Rejoice, the Lord Is King," drawn from his wider poetic corpus. All these hymns can enhance our experience of Lent and Easter.

We can trace the origins of Lent (the word itself simply means spring) to early Christian practice. The season began as a time of preparation for candidates who were to be baptized during the church's celebration of the Resurrection at Easter. The period of prayer, fasting, and instruction evolved into a season that all Christians observed so as to be better prepared to remember the crucifixion, death, and resurrection of Jesus. The forty days of Lent mirrored Jesus' forty days in the wilderness, that time of preparation for the beginning of his ministry. But the number forty had long symbolized particular times and events in which God prepared people of faith for service and deeper levels of commitment and witness. The Sundays during the season of Lent are not included because they all celebrate resurrection. So Lent always begins on Ash Wednesday and includes the important commemorations of Holy Week, particularly Maundy Thursday (when Jesus gave the new commandment to his disciples to love one another—"Maundy" comes from the Latin word *mandatum,* which means mandate or command), Good Friday (remembering the crucifixion), and Holy Saturday (to ponder the entombment of Jesus). In some traditions, the period from that Thursday evening through the Easter Vigil on Saturday evening and early Easter morning is known as the Easter Triduum.

The earliest Christians observed Pascha, or Christian Passover, in the spring of the year. Adapted from the Jewish festival of Passover, this sacred time commemorated both the crucifixion and resurrection of Jesus and the way in which God has redeemed us by grace through these events. Early Jewish Christians may have continued the celebration of both Pesach (Jewish Passover) and Pascha, but the expansion of Christianity into the Gentile world led to a singular commemoration of the crucifixion on Good Friday and of the Resurrection on the Sunday following. Easter, like Passover, is a movable feast based on the lunar calendar. The vast majority of Christians celebrate Easter on the first Sunday following the first full moon after the vernal equinox. So the date of Easter can range from March 22 to April 25, but the season of Lent is always the same length each year. A special place is given to the Octave of Easter, the eight-day period from Easter through the following Sunday. The Wesleys generally practiced daily Communion through this high and holy commemoration of Jesus' resurrection. These special days and seasons provide a means to shape sacred time. They provide a structure to help us remember the mighty acts of God and to respond reverently and faithfully to God's offer of relationship and love.

This special way of marking time, therefore, provides a unique opportunity to draw inspiration from the Bible and from the lyrical creations of a great theologian of the Anglican Communion. Culminating in Holy Week and the eight days of the Easter Octave, the themes of this sacred period focus our attention on the death and resurrection—the cross and our new creation in Christ. A Lenten discipline of study and reflection helps us take a journey inward and upward through these days, to face the reality of brokenness in life, and to reconnect with the "Friend of Sinners" who offers redemption, liberation, and grace to all. Walking with Christ through the days of Holy Week and experiencing anew the joy of the Resurrection throughout the Octave of Easter reminds us of who we are and to whom we belong as God's beloved children. The readings and Wesleyan hymns for each day in this study are arranged around these weekly Lenten themes:

- The Way of the Pilgrim
- Out of the Depths
- Friend of Sinners
- Groaning for Redemption
- God's Gift of Liberation
- Rejoicing in Grace

For Holy Week, we'll focus on the theme "Never Love Like His" and for the Octave of Easter, we'll turn to the theme "Break Forth into Praise!"

How to Use This Book

The season of Lent begins on Ash Wednesday and continues for forty days (not including Sundays) prior to the celebration of Easter. Although the Feast of the Resurrection falls on a different Sunday each year, the Lenten season of preparation leading through Holy Week, and the remembrance of Jesus' Crucifixion and Resurrection, always remains the same length. Throughout the history of the church, the first eight days of the Easter season, ending on the Second Sunday of Easter and known as the Octave of Easter, celebrate the central event of the Christian faith. This devotional manual—for use during the Season of Lent and the Octave of Easter—includes readings for the forty-six days of Lent and the eight days of the Octave.

Each of the readings includes a biblical text, a Wesley hymn selection, a brief meditation, and a prayer for the day. The devotional exercise begins, appropriately, in the Word of God. You'll find an index of Scripture Sources at the end of the book so you can see the range of Bible passages at a single glance. The hymns of Charles Wesley are arranged around appropriate themes for the seasons and are keyed to the scriptural texts proper to each day. The name of a hymn tune recommended for singing the text, as well as the title of a standard hymn sung to the same or similar meter, accompanies each hymn, if appropriate. These suggestions are drawn from *The Hymnal 1982* of The Episcopal Church (U.S.A.) but the hymn tunes and meters can be located in the index of the standard hymnals of many traditions.

The meters of the hymns and the suggested tunes are also collected in an index at the end of the book.

I have altered some of the hymn texts, substituting modern forms for archaic eighteenth-century English conventions. This applies particularly to elisions and spelling (for example, "choir" has replaced "quire," and "ancient" has replaced "antient"). I have also "Americanized" typical English spelling, replacing "Saviour," for example, with "Savior." Wherever appropriate, I have replaced "thee" and "thine" with "you" and "your" or have otherwise suitably updated the text. Occasionally I have retained Wesley's elisions, to clarify the meter or help those who sing the texts. Rarely, to make the hymns more user-friendly, I have taken some poetic license with the texts so that they conform more easily to the meter and flow of contemporary hymn tunes. Whenever I have changed the original, I hope I have not altered Wesley's meaning or fine poetic diction.

I am strongly committed to the use of inclusive language in all my writing and teaching. So one of the issues I struggle with is Wesley's use of masculine language for humanity. Wherever I noted possible changes for the purpose of inclusivity that were not destructive to the flow of the text I have made them. In those hymns where it was necessary, in my judgment, to retain the original "gendered" language of Wesley's poetry, I pray that this does not prove to be an insurmountable barrier to the truth and wisdom of his words. Whenever you encounter gender-exclusive references, I invite you to break out of these images; you may even want to attempt a new rendering of the text that retains the poetic form but is more sensitive to inclusivity. Charles Wesley was more concerned about a healthy and vital relationship with God than he was troubled by the language we use in our prayer. The emphasis on relationship strengthens Wesley's poetry, but even such an amazing wordsmith at that time could not appreciate fully how gendered language shapes our basic understandings. Authentic prayer awakens sensitivity, but the Spirit intercedes when language falters and fails.

Take time with the hymns. Meditate on them. Ponder the deep meaning of the words as they relate to God's offer of redemption and resurrected life in Christ, for the world and for you. The brief meditation and prayer provide a focus for reflection that I hope will lead to action.

Part Three of this book provides a pattern of either Morning or
Evening Prayer into which you may insert these devotional materials
as part of a longer liturgical observance. These formats are particularly suitable for corporate/parish prayer, group use, or an expanded
individual plan of spiritual formation through these seasons. The
purpose of these readings is to enrich your pilgrimage through Lent
to the glorious celebration of the Resurrection and to provide a means
by which individuals, families, discipleship groups, parishes and con-
gregations may live and sing "the song forever new."

PART ONE

Hymns and Prayers for Lent

FIRST DAYS OF LENT: THE WAY OF A PILGRIM

ASH WEDNESDAY

Read

Beware of practicing your piety before others in order to be seen by them; for then you have no reward from your Father in heaven. So whenever you give alms, do not sound a trumpet before you, as the hypocrites do in the synagogues and in the streets, so that they may be praised by others. Truly I tell you, they have received their reward. But when you give alms, do not let your left hand know what your right hand is doing, so that your alms may be done in secret; and your Father who sees in secret will reward you openly. And whenever you pray, do not be like the hypocrites; for they love to stand and pray in the synagogues and at the street corners, so that they may be seen by others. Truly I tell you, they have received their reward. But whenever you pray, go into your room and shut the door and pray to your Father who is in secret; and your Father who sees in secret will reward you. (Matthew 6:1–6)

1

Sing

Meter: 77.77

This hymn can be sung to "The Call," the tune used for "Come, my Way, my Truth, my Life."

Holy Lamb, who thee confess,
Followers of thy holiness,
Thee they ever keep in view,
Ever ask,—What shall we do?

Governed by thine only will,
All thy words we would fulfill,
Would in all thy footsteps go,
Walk as Jesus walked below.

While thou didst on earth appear,
Servant to thy servants here,
Mindful of thy place above,
All thy life was prayer and love.

Such our whole employment be,
Works of faith and charity,
Works of love on us bestowed,
Secret intercourse with God.

Early in the temple met
Let us still our Maker greet,
Nightly to the mount repair,
Join our praying pattern there:

There by wrestling faith obtain
Power to work for God again,
Power his image to retrieve,
Power like thee our Lord to live.

Vessels, instruments of grace,
Pass we thus our happy days

'Twixt the mount and multitude,
Doing, or receiving good:

Glad to pray, and labor on,
'Till our earthly course is run,
'Till we on the sacred tree
Bow the head, and die like thee.
                    (*Family Hymns*, Hymn 42)

Reflect

Faithful Christians have practiced Lent for countless generations.
The forty days of the season remind us of Jesus' sojourn in the wilderness and his struggle to know who he was and what his life's mission would be. The disciplines of the Lenten journey invite us into the
same process of discovery. We know that the confirmations and commitments from Jesus' time in the desert ultimately led to a cross. For
us to remain faithful to our calling as his disciples means, as Dietrich
Bonhoeffer reminded us so poignantly, that we too must take up our
cross and die. But if we have died with Christ, we know that we will
be united with him in his resurrection. Through baptism, God has
incorporated us into these mighty actions and this amazing narrative
of love. While our journey begins in ashes, it concludes in the joyous
affirmation of God's life-renewing power. Through it all, we seek to
walk as Jesus walked.

Prayer is the primary discipline of the journey that leads from Ash
Wednesday to the celebration of Jesus' resurrection and beyond. In a
hymn that Charles Wesley wrote specifically with families in mind, he
describes the pattern of prayer that Jesus lived. He maintains that "all
[his] life was prayer and love." He talks about the importance of holding faith and love together—about how our secret communion with
God in prayer is most fully realized in works of love and mercy for
others. He describes the importance of meeting with God regularly in
morning and evening devotions. A life of prayer—modeled after that
of Christ—he concludes, will be lived out "'Twixt the mount and multitude." What a marvelous image! We live out our lives as instruments
of grace, in the continual movement between lofty spiritual awaken-
ings and engagement with people—between moments in which we

glimpse the glory of God and times in which we love and give and serve others for the glory of God.

The sixth stanza of the hymn provides a vision of the goal toward which we move in our journey of faith, and while it was not composed with this season in mind, it connects so well with Lent. Being purposeful about rediscovering who we are and what God calls us to do with our lives empowers us to live like Christ, to work for God again, and to find God's image restored in our lives. This journey inward, upward, and outward involves serious soul-searching and risk-taking, honest reflection and courageous action. As Jesus' words in the Gospel reading for Ash Wednesday remind us, there is no place for self-righteousness in our quest to draw closer to God and to others. But God is faithful and will never leave us! And God's grace abounds! Let God mobilize your prayer into action. Take courage. Embrace your true identity and calling and you will be amazed by the ways the Spirit will shape you more and more into a beloved child of God.

Pray

Gracious God, as we take our first steps in this journey through the season of Lent, renew our vision of who we are and what you are calling us to do, through the power of the Spirit of Christ. Amen.

THURSDAY

Read

Whenever you fast, do not look dismal, like the hypocrites, for they disfigure their faces so as to show others that they are fasting. Truly I tell you, they have received their reward. But when you fast, put oil on your head and wash your face, so that your fasting may be seen not by others but by your Father who is in secret; and your Father who sees in secret will reward you. Do not store up for yourselves treasures on earth, where moth and rust consume and where thieves break in and steal; but store up for yourselves treasures in heaven, where neither moth nor rust consumes and where thieves do not break in and steal. For where your treasure is, there your heart will be also. (Matthew 6:16–21)

Sing

Meter: 886.886

This hymn can be sung to "Cornwall," the tune used for "We Sing of God, the Mighty Source."

How happy is the pilgrim's lot,
How free from every anxious thought,
From worldly hope and fear!
Confined to neither court nor cell,
My soul disdains on earth to dwell,
I only sojourn here.

My happiness in part is mine,
Already saved from self-design,
From every creature-love;
Blessed with the scorn of finite good,
My soul is lightened of its load,
And seeks the things above.

The things eternal I pursue,
A happiness beyond the view
Of those that basely pant
For things by nature felt and seen;
Their honors, wealth, and pleasures mean,
I neither have nor want.

I have no sharer of my heart,
To rob my Savior of a part,
And desecrate the whole:
Only betrothed to Christ am I,
And wait his coming from the sky,
To wed my happy soul.

No foot of land do I possess,
No cottage in this wilderness;
A poor wayfaring one,
I lodge a while in tents below,
Or gladly wander to and fro,
Till I my Canaan gain.

Nothing on earth I call my own,
A stranger, to the world unknown,
     I all their goods despise,
I trample on their whole delight,
And seek a country out of sight,
     A country in the skies.

There is my house and portion fair,
My treasure and my heart is there,
     And my abiding home;
For me my fellow pilgrims stay,
And angels beckon me away,
     And Jesus bids me come.

I come, your servant, Lord, replies,
I come to meet you in the skies,
     And claim my heavenly rest:
Now let the pilgrim's journey end,
Now, O my Savior, brother, friend,
     Receive me to your breast.
          (*Redemption Hymns*, Hymn 51.1–4, 6–9)

Reflect

Most people associate Lent with sacrifices of one form or another. People give up all sorts of things from chocolate to television during this season, and well they should. Sacrifices of this type, no matter how small, free the spirit and reconnect us with an important aspect of authentic Christian living. In a world where so many die each day of hunger, the sacrifice of a meal reminds those of us with plenty that God has blessed us richly and desires for all to live fully. In a culture where the media shapes our values, goals, and dreams, it is important to escape from the constant bombardment of ads and images, and to abide in the biblical vision of life in Christ. Even the abandonment of one simple pleasure during this journey can remind us of God's call to seek God's dominion first—to fix our eyes upon Jesus and his way in the world.

Wesley's hymn provides images counter to the seductive values of materialism and consumerism. He does little more than paraphrase

Jesus' bold proclamation in the Sermon on the Mount. Don't we all need to hear this message again? Particularly in this culture, in this time in history? As we lighten our load at the outset of this journey to the cross we are reminded to store up treasures in heaven, to invest in those things that are truly eternal. The authentic disciple, claims Wesley, despises material gain in this world and tramples on the worldly delight in things. He understands how the things we tend to cling to in this life for security can weigh us down and claim our ultimate allegiance. We can actually begin to believe that our happiness depends upon pleasure, wealth, and honor; that we have earned the treasures we accumulate as the products of our own labor, rather than viewing all as the gifts of God's grace.

On January 1, 1953, a pacifist and peace activist by the name of Mildred Norman began a twenty-eight year walking pilgrimage that would carry her across the United States nearly seven times. Adopting the name "Peace Pilgrim," she vowed to remain a wanderer until humanity learned the way of peace. She walked until she was given shelter and fasted until she was offered food. She carried no money and owned nothing except for the clothes on her back. She claimed that she never went wanting a day in her life over the course of three decades. One of the lessons she learned as a consequence of her pilgrimage was that de-accumulating her possessions liberated her. Her sacrifices, to use the language of Wesley, freed her "from every anxious thought, from worldly hope and fear!" Freedom from things enabled her to focus on God and others.

In all probability, none of us will live with the same kind of prophetic zeal or reckless abandon that characterized the practice of Peace Pilgrim—nor could we—but we can begin to taste the liberation of which she speaks in our own lives, this Lent, if we have the courage to live as those who take sacrifice seriously.

Pray

Self-giving God, help us not to cling to things as if our security and happiness were dependent upon them; rather, give us the will and the courage to store up treasures in heaven, to invest our lives first and foremost in the realization of your reign in this world. Amen.

FRIDAY

Read

Not that I have already obtained this or have already reached the goal; but I press on to make it my own, because Christ Jesus has made me his own. Beloved, I do not consider that I have made it my own; but this one thing I do: forgetting what lies behind and straining forward to what lies ahead, I press on towards the goal for the prize of the heavenly call of God in Christ Jesus. Brothers and sisters, join in imitating me, and observe those who live according to the example you have in us. For many live as enemies of the cross of Christ; I have often told you of them, and now I tell you even with tears. Their end is destruction; their god is the belly; and their glory is in their shame; their minds are set on earthly things. But our citizenship is in heaven, and it is from there that we are expecting a Savior, the Lord Jesus Christ. He will transform the body of our humiliation so that it may be conformed to the body of his glory, by the power that also enables him to make all things subject to himself. (Philippians 3:12–14, 17–21)

Sing

Meter: 888.888

This hymn can be sung to "Old 113th," the tune used for "I'll Praise My Maker While I've Breath."

> Leader of faithful souls, and guide
>   Of all that travel to the sky,
> Come, and with us, e'en us abide,
>   Who would on you alone rely,
> On you alone our spirits stay,
> While held in life's uneven way.
>
> Strangers and pilgrims here below,
>   This earth, we know, is not our place,
> And hasten through the vale of woe,
>   And restless to behold your face,
> Swift to our heavenly country move,
> Our everlasting home above.

We have no 'biding city here,
    But seek a city out of sight;
Thither our steady course we steer,
    Aspiring to the plains of light,
Jerusalem, the saints' abode,
Whose founder is the living God.

Patient th'appointed race to run,
    This weary world we cast behind,
From strength to strength we travel on,
    The New Jerusalem to find,
Our labor this, our only aim,
To find the New Jerusalem.

Through you, who all our sins has borne,
    Freely and graciously forgiven,
With songs to Zion we return,
    Contending for our native heaven,
That palace of our glorious King,
We find it nearer while we sing.

Raised by the breath of love divine,
    We urge our way with strength renewed,
The church of the first-born to join,
    We travel to the mount of God,
With joy upon our heads arise,
And meet our Captain in the skies.
            (*Redemption Hymns*, Hymn 41.1–4, 6, 8)

Reflect

Paul's Letter to the Philippians provides amazing insights into the nature of our Christian pilgrimage. From a prison cell in Rome, the apostle reminds his beloved community that heaven is their true home. The goal of this pilgrim journey is to glorify and live with God forever. Paul wants to make sure his followers understand that nothing glorifies God more than the unbroken fellowship we share with God through Christ. While based upon God's grace, this relationship, like all relationships, requires vigilant attention. We can be distracted easily from the goal, particularly by those Paul describes as the "enemies of the cross of Christ." They delight in pleasure ("their god is the belly"), take pride in unrighteousness ("their glory is in their shame"), and fall prey to consumerism ("their minds are set on earthly things"). In the midst of the journey, it is important to keep our eyes fixed, therefore, on the ultimate goal.

Charles Wesley picks up this theme in one of his most effective "pilgrim hymns." He contrasts the eternal home toward which we move with life's uneven way, describing this weary world as a vale of woe. Perhaps he echoes here the ancient prayer *Salve Regina*: "To you, O Lord, we send up our sighs, mourning and weeping in this vale of tears." You can feel the weight, sense the darkness, and empathize, as Paul does, with the misery of those who have not yet perceived the true meaning of it all. The power of this hymn, however, resides in its increasing pace and the magnetic attraction of the finish line toward which we move. The pilgrim race begins with an invitation to Christ as guide. Patience and steadiness characterize the initial steps in the journey as we become more secure in our footing. Like the disciple Christian in John Bunyan's classic, *Pilgrim's Progress*, we do not let barriers and detours deter us from our goal. These obstacles, in fact, serve to quicken our pace as we resist their pull. With each new victory we begin to travel "from strength to strength" toward the New Jerusalem where all the saints await. They cheer us here below. The singing of the community draws us closer and closer still. Ultimately, we meet our Captain—Jesus, the pioneer and perfecter of our faith—"in the skies." As we look back over the course of the pilgrimage completed—the race won—we immediately see that we were "raised by the breath of love divine." What an amazing vision of the life we live in Christ.

Does this "race" to heaven diminish the importance of life in the here and now? Absolutely not! In both creation and in God's act of entering human history in the person of Jesus Christ, God declares that this life is good. God calls us to journey through life with Christ, not to run away from it. But the race calls for a realistic vision. The abiding lesson is clear: Keep your eye fixed on the goal. Embrace the good that surrounds you day in and day out. Do not be seduced or overcome by the darkness that is also a part of life.

Pray

Compassionate Guide and Friend, even as we send up our sighs, mourning and weeping in this vale of tears, help us to keep our eyes firmly fixed upon the goal of our high calling in Jesus Christ, the pioneer and perfecter of our faith. Amen.

SATURDAY

Read

I therefore, the prisoner in the Lord, beg you to lead a life worthy of the calling to which you have been called, with all humility and gentleness, with patience, bearing with one another in love, making every effort to maintain the unity of the Spirit in the bond of peace. There is one body and one Spirit, just as you were called to the one hope of your calling, one Lord, one faith, one baptism, one God and Father of all, who is above all and through all and in all. But each of us was given grace according to the measure of Christ's gift. The gifts he gave were that some would be apostles, some prophets, some evangelists, some pastors and teachers, to equip the saints for the work of ministry, for building up the body of Christ, until all of us come to the unity of the faith and of the knowledge of the Son of God, to maturity, to the measure of the full stature of Christ. (Ephesians 4:1–7, 11–13)

Sing

Meter: CMD

This hymn can be sung to "Forest Green," the tune used for "I Sing the Almighty Power of God."

> All praise to our redeeming Lord,
>   Who joins us by his grace,
> And bids us, each to each restored,
>   Together seek his face.
> He bids us build each other up,
>   And gathered into one;
> To our high calling's glorious hope
>   We hand in hand go on.

The gift which he on one bestows
 We all delight to prove,
The grace through every vessel flows
 In purest streams of love.
E'en now we speak, and think the same,
 And cordially agree,
Concentered all through Jesus' name
 In perfect harmony.

We all partake the joy of one,
 The common peace we feel,
A peace to sensual minds unknown,
 A joy unspeakable.
And if our fellowship below
 In Jesus be so sweet,
What height of rapture shall we know,
 When round his throne we meet.
   (*Redemption Hymns*, Hymn 32)

Reflect

Two words leap out of both text and hymn: "one" and "calling." In the Epistle to the Ephesians, the author explores the theme of Christian unity and connects it intimately to the high calling of Christian disciples in the one Lord, Jesus. In this brief selection of verses, the word "one" appears no fewer than eight times. Wesley translates the rather lofty theological language of the letter into very intimate, personal, and relational images. The common experience of God's grace in life—something always deeply relational for the Wesleys—joins all together as one. Rather than conceiving grace as a thing, Charles and his brother view grace essentially as God's offer of relationship. It empowers the believer to trust, love, and serve God, which, in turn, restores our capacity to serve and love others. God's loving embrace takes us all in and makes us one. Drawing close to God moves us all closer to one another. As we journey together, not only are we reconciled to God, but we experience the restoration of relationships with our companions as well. Unity in Christ builds up the community. We go on "hand in hand" toward "our high calling's glorious hope." What a profoundly intimate portrait of life in the company of Jesus' followers. So we never make this pilgrimage alone: we are surrounded by companions throughout the course of the journey—the Triune God, the great cloud of witnesses or communion of saints, and our fellow pilgrims here and now.

We have encountered a number of pilgrimage images these past days, related both to Lent and life. They are encapsulated in action verbs: Walk. Sacrifice. Run. Strain. Our readings for today point us toward another image that deals with our calling as faithful Gospel-bearers, namely, "march." The particular forms of pilgrimage that come immediately to my mind in this regard, since I am a product of the 1950s, are the many marches for civil rights that I witnessed as a child. My father was deeply committed to this struggle. So he made sure we took advantage of every opportunity to know about the events of those days, and even to meet some of the great leaders in the march toward freedom like Dr. Martin Luther King, Jr., whom I met as a little boy. I can still play the images in my mind. Men and women, linked arm in arm, singing the songs of freedom. In the face of prejudice, hatred, and animosity, they stretched forward to see "the glory of the coming of the Lord." Nothing moves us closer to our heavenly home than engagement in acts of justice and compassion here in this world. Courageous action of this kind—reflecting our commitment to God's reign or peaceable kingdom—requires a community. It may not be too much to claim that the community of God's people, singing, "We are marching in the light of God," walking together hand in hand, brought the evil walls of apartheid crumbling to the ground. As Wesley attests, this journey brings unknown peace and unspeakable joy to those who have the courage to join in.

Pray

God of justice and peace, we never have to make our journey toward you alone. Not only are you with us always, but you gather us into a community of fellow pilgrims. Help us to reach out our hands to those around us and to celebrate the march of freedom in Christ. Amen.

LENT I: OUT OF THE DEPTHS

THE FIRST SUNDAY IN LENT

Read

Out of the depths I cry to you, O Lord. Lord, hear my voice! Let your ears be attentive to the voice of my supplications! If you, O Lord, should mark iniquities, Lord, who could stand? But there is forgiveness with you, so that you may be revered. I wait for the Lord, my soul waits, and in his word I hope; my soul waits for the Lord more than those who watch for the morning, more than those who watch for the morning. (Psalm 130:1–6)

Sing

Meter: 77.77.77

This hymn can be sung to "Toplady," the tune used for "Rock of Ages Cleft for Me."

From the depths I cry, O Lord,
Hear my supplicating word,
Hast'ning to eternal death,
Jesus, Lord, I cry to thee,
Help a feeble child of earth,
Show forth all thy power in me.

Only you can hear my call,
Blessed Savior, friend of all:
Well thou knowest my desperate case,
Thou my curse of sin remove,
Save me by thy richest grace,
Save me by thy pardoning love.

How shall I thy mercy find,
Savior, bless'd, of humankind!
Canst thou not accept my prayer,
Not bestow the grace I claim?

Where are thy old mercies, where
    All the powers of Jesus' name?

    Can I find the words to move
      All the mercies of thy love?
Are they not already stirred?
    Have I in thy death no part?
Ask thine own compassions, Lord,
    Ask the yearnings of thy heart!

    I will never let thee go,
      Till I all thy mercy know:
Let me hear the welcome sound,
    Speak, if still thou canst forgive,
Speak, and let the lost be found,
    Speak, and let the dying live.

    Thy dear love is all my plea,
      Lord, thy cross speaks out for me:
By thy pangs and bloody sweat,
    By thy depth of grief unknown,
Save me gasping at thy feet,
    Save, O save thy ransomed one!

    What hast thou now done for me,
      Think, O Lord, on Calvary!
By thy mortal groans, and sighs,
    By thy precious death I pray,
Hear my dying spirit's cries,
    Take, O take my sins away!
        (*Redemption Hymns*,
    Hymn 29, altered from 66.77.77)

Reflect

At a very critical point in my life a good friend reminded me that one of the secrets to true happiness was coming to know and learning to live within your limitations. That was a hard lesson but an important one and it helped me recover a proper perspective.

We are not far into our Lenten pilgrimage before a much more disturbing reality confronts us head on. The Psalmist shakes us from the delusion of any false sense of security we may have in ourselves. "Out of the depths I cry to you, O Lord." When faced with the reality of who God is—the Creator who both knows and loves us through and through—our immediate response is the same as Isaiah in the temple or Simon Peter in the boat. We are awestruck by the tremendous majesty of God and the realization of how far we are from God's intentions for us. We know that our lips are unclean. We fall on our faces, recognizing our failures and impotence. "If you, O Lord, should mark iniquities," the Psalmist confesses, "Lord, who could stand?"

Charles Wesley displays a profound sense of urgency concerning this state of alienation—this distance from God. He considers it to be a matter of life and death. Like the great medieval theologian Anselm of Canterbury, he acknowledges that we must consider the heavy weight of sin if we are ever going to experience genuine fellowship with God. Despite the fact that we are God's children, we are feeble. Our situation is desperate. We are lost. The realization of our condition triggers an unrelenting series of questions. Am I too far gone for God to accept my prayer? Is God no longer merciful? What will it take for God to hear and respond to my desperate yearning for reconciliation and peace? We gasp at the feet of Jesus, pleading, listening for some word of hope. "Let me hear the welcome sound," Charles sings. Note the potent repetition of the petition for God to "speak." As in creation, so in the miracle of re-creation, God's words—God's speech—God's song—lifts us from these depths. Speak, if you can still forgive me. Speak, and lead me home by the sound of your voice. Speak, and transform my death into newness of life.

If we are honest with ourselves, we know that we are utterly lost without Christ. We do not love God with our whole heart. We break God's laws and rebel against God's love. We do not love our neighbors and we close our ears to the cries of the needy. Out of these depths, we cry to God, and our healing begins when we acknowledge the fact that we are broken, fallen, and lost. Like the addict who yearns for health and wholeness, we need to take the first step and say to God, "I am as you find me, but this is not who I want to be. Change me." In the midst of that darkness, we cry with the Psalmist, "my soul waits for the Lord more than those who watch for the morning." We trust that the light will dawn.

Pray

O Lord, out of the deep we cry to you, acknowledging our failure to be your faithful children: Help us to wait for you more than those who watch for the morning and to place our hope in your word. Amen.

MONDAY IN LENT I

Read

Have mercy on me, O God, according to your steadfast love; according to your abundant mercy blot out my transgressions. Wash me thoroughly from my iniquity, and cleanse me from my sin. For I know my transgressions, and my sin is ever before me. Against you, you alone, have I sinned, and done what is evil in your sight, so that you are justified in your sentence and blameless when you pass judgment. Indeed, I was born guilty, a sinner when my mother conceived me. You desire truth in the inward being; therefore teach me wisdom in my secret heart. Purge me with hyssop, and I shall be clean; wash me, and I shall be whiter than snow. Let me hear joy and gladness; let the bones that you have crushed rejoice. Hide your face from my sins, and blot out all my iniquities. Create in me a clean heart, O God, and put a new and right spirit within me. Do not cast me away from your presence, and do not take your holy spirit from me. . . . O Lord, open my lips, and my mouth will declare your praise. For you have no delight in sacrifice; if I were to give a burnt-offering, you would not be pleased. The sacrifice acceptable to God is a broken spirit; a broken and contrite heart, O God, you will not despise. (Psalm 51:1–11, 15–17)

Sing

Meter: LM

This hymn can be sung to "Dickinson College," the tune used for "Lord, Make Us Servants of Your Peace."

> Eternal power of Jesu's name,
> > For thee with broken heart I cry,

Savior from sin, from fear, from shame,
  Come down, or I forever die!

Thy only name can be my balm,
  My spirit's desperate sickness heal,
Thy only voice the storm can calm,
  And bid my troubled heart be still.

If yet thou canst compassion have,
  If grace doth more than sin abound,
Exert thine utmost power to save,
  And let me in thy rest be found.

Lay to thy hand, almighty love,
  The work, O God, is worthy thee,
Such huge destruction to remove,
  And save a soul so lost as me!

Th'intolerable load sustain,
  Th'inextricable knot untie,
Loose the indissoluble chain,
  And show thyself the Lord most high.

Nor can my desperate heart conceive
  How God himself should save so far:
But humbly all to him I leave,
  If yet he will his power declare.

Dying in sin, condemned, and lost,
  I cast me on a God unknown,
And cry, while rendering up the ghost,
  Thy will, thy only will be done!
              (*Redemption Hymns*,
          Hymn 45.1–3, 5–6, 9–10)

Reflect

Lost! For many of us that word conjures up images of desperation on what would seem to be a God-forsaken island. Is that a modern day parable of life? Psalm 51 reminds us of our lost condition. Regardless of what the sin was that led the Psalmist to pray for mercy and cleansing with such passion, the penitent author provides us with a vocabulary for repentance and opens the windows of the soul to God's cleansing and healing Spirit. The Psalmist not only asks for a thorough washing that removes the film of outward sin, but confesses the need for a deep, inward cleansing that involves nothing less than a total transformation from the inside out. The heart, of course, functions as a metaphor for that deepest part of our being where we nourish our fears and nurture our hates. Only God's work on the heart can satisfy our longing to be whole and free. Psalm 51 is first and foremost a prayer about the human heart.

Martin Luther talked often about the heart turned in on itself. Like his theological mentor, Augustine, he too believed that the loves of the human being are disordered. We should love the Lord our God with our whole heart, mind, soul, and strength. But instead of loving God with that kind of affection or devotion, we use God as a means to our own ends. Rather than placing God first in all things, self reigns upon the altar of the human heart, and this original sin distorts every aspect of who we are and what we do. As long as our affections are disordered in this way, genuine love of God, others, and self remains elusive. Wesley describes the heart, therefore, as broken, troubled, and desperate, because that is exactly how we feel in this condition. He relates these potent adjectives to three images that hit us with particular force. An "intolerable load" weighs us down. An "inextricable knot" ties us up. Ponder those images. Nothing seems to be able to extricate us from the "indissoluble chain" of sin and death that binds our hearts and burdens our minds.

The only remedy for our sin, fear, and shame is God's restorative act, powerfully symbolized in the Sacrament of Baptism. Of all the images associated with this sign-act of God's love through the church, perhaps none resonates more with us than the cleansing power of water. I once heard a wise disciple describe the interesting way in which God makes Christians. Unlike the local club that extends a hand of welcome and a slap on the back, the church says, "You are dirty. You need to be cleaned up. Come to the water. We'll give you a new name and God will give you a new heart." In the waters of Baptism we are born anew to a living hope.

Permit all these images to flood your heart and mind each day as you begin Morning and Evening Prayer with the words of today's Psalm: "O Lord, open my lips, and my mouth will declare your praise." Make the prayer of the Psalmist your prayer this day.

Pray

O Lord, open my lips, and my mouth will declare your praise, for despite the fact that I am undone and come to you in need of a great washing and cleansing in my life, you have promised to create a clean heart in me and to put a new and right spirit within me. Amen.

TUESDAY IN LENT I

Read

I will sprinkle clean water upon you, and you shall be clean from all your uncleannesses, and from all your idols I will cleanse you. A new heart I will give you, and a new spirit I will put within you; and I will remove from your body the heart of stone and give you a heart of flesh. I will put my spirit within you, and make you follow my statutes and be careful to observe my ordinances. Then you shall live in the land that I gave to your ancestors; and you shall be my people, and I will be your God. (Ezekiel 36:25–28)

Sing

Meter: LM

This hymn can be sung to "Hereford," the tune used for "O Thou Who Camest from Above."

> What shall I do my God to love,
>> My God, who loved, and died for me?
> Obdurate heart, will nothing move,
>> Will nothing melt or soften thee?
>
> Jesus, thou lovely bleeding Lamb,
>> To thee I pour out my complaint:

I cannot hide from thee my shame,
    I own, and blush to own my want.

I want a heart to love my God,
    I cannot bear this heart of stone:
Soften it, Savior, by thy blood,
    And melt the nether millstone down.

The stone cries out, I do not love,
    And breaks my heart its want to own,
The mountain now begins to move,
    And half relents my heart of stone.

Thou lov'dst, before the world began,
    This poor unloving soul of mine:
Jesus came down, my God was man,
    That I might all become divine.

My anchor this, which cannot move,
    The servant as his Lord shall be,
And I shall live my God to love,
    And die for him who died for me.
                (*Redemption Hymns,*
                Hymn 43.1–3, 6, 9–10)

Reflect

The prophet Ezekiel provides another perspective related to the heart work required to make us God's own, and Wesley amplifies his primary image. He contrasts the heart of stone with the heart of flesh. Note how Wesley describes this heart set against God. He uses language heard infrequently today and needing some explanation. An "obdurate heart" cannot be moved by persuasion, pity, or tender feelings. It stubbornly resists moral influence, remaining persistently impenitent. Wesley compares this heart of stone to a "nether millstone," the lower of two millstones used in grinding grain into flour. This lower stone must be immoveable and extremely hard so as to bear the weight of the stone on top that does the work of milling the grain. Could there be a harsher image? Is it possible for a heart to become so callused and cold? Is there nothing that can melt or soften such a heart of stone? If we are brutally honest with ourselves, does this not describe our hearts, hardened by life, weighed down by disappointment, compressed by failure, shame, and self-accusation? Where has your own heart become cold and hard in relation to other people and to God?

Look closely at stanza four of the hymn, for it signals the true nature of repentance from a Wesleyan perspective. The stone—the heart—cries out, "I do not love." John Wesley one time defined repentance as true self-understanding. I am certain that he drew this vision of repentance from the parable of the prodigal son. As in this hymn, the critical turning point for the prodigal comes in the narrative where it says, "he came to himself." When our hearts "come to themselves," when we acknowledge the obdurate nature of our wills and desires, at that moment the heart breaks and the healing begins. "The mountain now begins to move," claims Wesley. The heart of stone begins to relent, and the healing process thus begun culminates in an amazing realization—one of God's greatest gifts to us. We realize that, despite our stony nature and despite the many times we have stood like a nether stone against God and God's way, God loves us still. In fact, there has never been a time, Wesley claims, when God has not loved "this poor unloving soul of mine." God's love reaches out to you and me even "before the world began."

Only love can heal an obdurate heart, but the extent of love's healing power overwhelms us. Wesley confesses with Athanasius that God became incarnate in Jesus—the divine became human—in order that we might become like him. When God heals our hearts of stone by replacing them with hearts of love, God begins the process of restoring the *imago Dei*—the image of God—in us. God begins the process of conforming our lives to the image of Christ. Ezekiel goes so far as to say that "you shall be clean from all your uncleannesses," and connects this life-restoring act of God with the Spirit. The broken hearted receive not only a new heart, but a new spirit as well.

Pray

Source of all healing and love, we acknowledge our hearts of stone and confess the many times we have preferred hardness of heart to your way of love; give us new hearts and put a new spirit within us so that we can be your people again, for the sake of Christ. Amen.

WEDNESDAY IN LENT I

Read

Fools say in their hearts, "There is no God." They are corrupt, they do abominable deeds; there is no one who does good. The Lord looks down from heaven on humankind to see if there are any who are wise, who seek after God. They have all gone astray, they are all alike perverse; there is no one who does good, no, not one. Have they no knowledge, all the evildoers who eat up my people as they eat bread, and do not call upon the Lord? There they shall be in great terror, for God is with the company of the righteous. You would confound the plans of the poor, but the Lord is their refuge. O that deliverance for Israel would come from Zion! When the Lord restores the fortunes of his people, Jacob will rejoice; Israel will be glad. (Psalm 14)

Sing

Meter: 66.66D

This hymn can be sung to "Gottes Sohn ist Kommen," repeating the first line of the tune used for "Once He Came in Blessing."

You simple souls, that stray
Far from the path of peace
(That unfrequented way
To life and happiness)
Why will you folly love,
And throng the downward road,
Hate wisdom from above,
And mock the sons of God?

Poor pensive sojourners,
O'erwhelmed with griefs and woes,

Perplexed with needless fears,
And pleasure's mortal foes;
Ensnared by gaping tomb
Our sight you cannot bear,
Wrapped in a dismal gloom
Of fanciful despair.

Riches unsearchable
In Jesus' love we know,
And pleasures from the well
Of life our souls o'erflow:
The Spirit we receive
Of wisdom, grace, and power,
Despite the sorrow live,
Rejoicing evermore.

Angels our servants are,
And keep in all our ways,
And in their hands they bear
The sacred sons of grace;
Our guides to heavenly bliss
They all our steps attend,
For God our Father is,
And Jesus is our friend.

With him we walk in white,
We in his image shine,
Our robes are robes of light,
Our righteousness divine:
On all the kings of earth
With pity we look down,
And claim our second birth,
A never-fading crown.

(*Redemption Hymns*,
Hymn 16.1, 3, 5–7)

Reflect

Folly often leads us in a downward spiral into the depths and away from God. A "foolish heart" can easily take control of a person's life.

How many foolish things have you done that have led you astray? What follies have you embraced that carried your life into places you wish now you had never gone? The Psalmist encapsulates the most critical form of foolishness in the simple statement, "Fools say in their hearts, 'There is no God.'" The root of all our problems, as Augustine claimed long ago, is the desire to be *sicut Dei*—like God. The account of the fall of humanity in the creation narrative of Genesis points to this very issue, and the heart controlled by this folly leads to all manner of sin. The Psalmist describes such people as corrupt, abominable, perverse. Their disease originates in their failure to recognize that we live our lives perennially *coram Deo*—before God. The term "fool," then, designates a person who decides and acts on the basis of this wrong assumption. Moreover, the Psalmist seems to imply that this ultimate foolishness characterizes all people. It is like a fatal flaw deep within us; the fact that we are created in God's image makes us want to be God, and that desire can dominate our lives. So the Psalmist laments: "The Lord looks down from heaven on humankind to see if there are any who are wise, who seek after God. They have all gone astray, they are all alike perverse; there is no one who does good, no, not one." We need wisdom, but we act like fools.

Wesley connects this issue of wisdom and folly with the human pilgrimage. The Lenten journey provides the perfect opportunity, therefore, to consider this matter in our own lives. The opening stanza of the hymn may remind you of Robert Frost's classic poem, "The road less traveled." As in the poem, so in life, the path we choose makes all the difference. According to Wesley, the road less traveled—the path to genuine life and happiness—is the way of peace. Like the Psalmist, he will not leave this discussion of wisdom and folly on a lofty, philosophical level. He brings it right down to earth. The problem is not a rational argument against the existence of God, but behavior based upon the assumption that we are not held accountable by God, with all the disastrous consequences that ensue. The foolish ones choose a "downward road," says Wesley, the seductive way of the masses. Their choices leave them pensive and perplexed, ensnared by death and wrapped in gloom. But there is an alternate route. Elsewhere the Psalmist observes that "the fear of the Lord is the beginning of wisdom" (111:10). The sacred scriptures also describe a close connection between Wisdom and the Word. The redemptive act of Christ mirrors the creative act of Wisdom. With the Wisdom/Word as our companion on the road less travelled, we encounter "riches unsearchable." Servants surround us with their constant care and guidance. We even dare to hope to shine one day in his image—the image of Christ.

Pray

Merciful God, we confess that we have often acted like foolish children, making decisions and behaving as if you had no place in our lives; teach us the way of wisdom that leads to peace so that we may stand before you as beloved and righteous children. Amen.

THURSDAY IN LENT I

Read

"Come to me, all you that are weary and are carrying heavy burdens, and I will give you rest. Take my yoke upon you, and learn from me; for I am gentle and humble in heart, and you will find rest for your souls. For my yoke is easy, and my burden is light." (Matthew 11:28–30)

Sing

Meter: 77.77D

This hymn can be sung to "Aberystwyth," the tune used for "Jesus, Lover of My Soul."

> Come, ye weary sinners, come,
>   All who groan to bear your load,
> Jesus calls his wanderers home;
>   Hasten to your pardoning God:
> Come, ye guilty spirits oppressed,
>   Answer to the Savior's call,
> "Come, and I will give you rest,
>   Come, and I will save you all."
>
> Jesus, full of truth and love,
>   We thy kindest word obey,
> Faithful let thy mercies prove,
>   Take our load of guilt away:

Now the promised rest bestow,
   Rest from servitude severe,
Rest from all our toil and woe,
   Rest from all our grief and fear.

Weary of this war within,
   Weary of this endless strife,
Weary of ourselves and sin,
   Weary of a wretched life;
Fain we would on thee rely,
   Cast on thee our sin and care,
To thy arms of mercy fly,
   Find our lasting quiet there.

Burdened with a world of grief,
   Burdened with our sinful load,
Burdened with this unbelief,
   Burdened with the wrath of God,
Lo! We come to thee for ease,
   True and gracious as thou art,
Now our groaning soul release,
   Write forgiveness on our heart.
         (*Redemption Hymns*, Hymn 10)

Reflect

Wesley provides a lyrical exposition of Jesus' words recorded in Matthew 11. We know the text well: "Come to me, all you that are weary and are carrying heavy burdens, and I will give you rest. Take my yoke upon you, and learn from me; for I am gentle and humble in heart, and you will find rest for your souls. For my yoke is easy, and my burden is light." We cannot hear those words enough.

The hymn includes one of Wesley's most masterful uses of anaphora, the literary device of repeating the same word at the beginning of consecutive lines. Rest. Weary. Burdened. He reverses the order of Jesus' words by first stating the deepest desire of the human heart—rest—before describing the human state—weary and burdened. As a consequence of this rearrangement, he draws us into the possibility of finding rest for both soul and body in the person of Jesus

Christ. He presents the promise first. He suggests the remedy before he offers his diagnosis, emphasizing God's prevenient action, God's desire to heal, and God's initiative rooted in grace.

Take some time to ponder the questions that Wesley poses.

What wears you down?

- War within—What are the battles you are presently waging internally?
- Endless strife—Is there some continual struggle in which you are involved?
- Ourselves and sin—What have you said or done that has alienated you from God and others and continues to eat at you?
- A wretched life—What is it that makes you feel depleted and unfulfilled?

What weighs heavy upon you in life?

- A world of grief—What losses have you sustained that continue to burden you?
- Our sinful load—What sins do you carry around with you every day?
- Unbelief—What makes it difficult for you to entrust your life to Christ?
- Fear of God's wrath—What stands between you and God that fills you with fear?

The rest that God offers in Christ is all encompassing. When we abide in Christ we are liberated from servitude, from toil and woe, from grief and fear. Wesley concludes with the astounding affirmation that forgiveness procures our rest. This act of God for us in Christ frees us from the burden of feeling we can never do enough to please God, others, or ourselves. It emancipates us from the weariness of our own efforts that are often life-depleting. It offers a balm for the pain of separation from God and others that characterizes life in this world. God "writes forgiveness on our hearts."

Pray

Forgiving God, we come to you weary and burdened and seeking rest from all those forces that deplete our lives: Help us to rest secure in the promise that you will give rest for our souls and free us for abundant life in Christ. Amen.

FRIDAY IN LENT I

Read

Thomas said to him, "Lord, we do not know where you are going. How can we know the way?" Jesus said to him, "I am the way, and the truth, and the life. No one comes to the Father except through me. If you know me, you will know my Father also. From now on you do know him and have seen him." Philip said to him, "Lord, show us the Father, and we will be satisfied." Jesus said to him, "Have I been with you all this time, Philip, and you still do not know me? Whoever has seen me has seen the Father. How can you say, 'Show us the Father'? Do you not believe that I am in the Father and the Father is in me? The words that I say to you I do not speak on my own; but the Father who dwells in me does his works. Believe me that I am in the Father and the Father is in me; but if you do not, then believe me because of the works themselves." (John 14:5–11)

Sing

Meter: 88.88.88

This hymn can be sung to "St. Petersburg," the tune used for "Before Thy Throne, O God."

O thou, whose Spirit hath made known
    My want of living faith divine,
Hear thy poor mournful captive groan,
    Now in my nature's darkness shine,
Now in mine inmost soul display
The glorious blaze of gospel day.

A stranger to thy people's joys,
    An alien from the life of grace,
I never heard thy pardoning voice,
    I never saw thy smiling face,

I never felt thy blood applied,
Or knew for me the Savior died.

Or if I did begin to taste
    The sweetness of redeeming love,
The momentary bliss is past,
    The tender joy no more I prove,
My faith is lost, my power is gone,
I sin, and have not Jesus known.

But wilt thou not at last appear,
    Object of all my wishful hope,
The conscious unbeliever cheer,
    And raise the fallen sinner up,
The God-revealing Spirit give,
And kindly help me to believe?

Thou only dost the Godhead know,
    Thou only canst to all reveal,
To me, to me the Father show,
    To me, to me the secret tell:
Now, Savior, now the veil remove,
And tell my heart, that God is love.

I will not let my sorrow go,
    Till Jesus wipes away my tears,
Kindly extorts the stubborn woe,
    And lastingly his mourner cheers;
Constrained to cry by love divine,
My God, thou art forever mine!
        (*Redemption Hymns*, Hymn 42.1–5, 8)

Reflect

A blatant honesty in today's texts strikes us rather sharply. The account of Thomas and Philip in the Gospel and Wesley's hymn concerning the singer's lack of living faith cut to the quick. The subjects in these scenes are lost, not because they have never known the truth or stood in the light; rather, despite the fact they have walked with

Jesus and experienced God's love through him, they still do not get it. What hits us so hard here is the fact that this could be you and me. An unavoidable reality confronts us and sends a shudder up and down our spine.

When darkness completely envelopes our lives, it is virtually impossible to find our way. Listen to Philip's request again. "Lord, show us the Father, and we will be satisfied." He says in effect, "Just give us some light, perhaps just a glimmer. We don't see clearly where we are or where we are going." You can hear the pain in Jesus' voice. "The light has been surrounding you all this time, and you still stumble in the darkness." God's light shines through this One who is completely transparent, but the disciples still do not have eyes to see. They just don't understand.

Charles Wesley loves to play with the images of darkness and light because they are so real to us in life. He alludes repeatedly in his hymns to "nature's darkness," referring to the sinful condition of all human beings. He contrasts life in this dark world with "the glorious blaze of gospel day." He describes those who dwell in darkness as strangers and aliens. His poetry is powerful and moving. We feel for the one who never heard, who never saw, who never felt. But more pathetic still is the one who began to taste, but the "momentary bliss is past." "My faith is lost," he laments, "my power is gone." Charles Wesley's older brother, John, one time wrote him a letter filled with such pathos. It came at a time when the success of his movement of Christian renewal was well secured. He wrote parts of the letter in a secret code so that only Charles would have access to his painful cry. "I do not love God," he confessed. "I never did. . . . I have no direct witness, I do not say that I am a child of God, but of anything invisible or eternal" (letter of June 27, 1766). He sounds very much like the plaintiff of Charles's hymn, abandoned to the dark night of the soul:

> My faith is lost, my power is gone,
> I sin, and have not Jesus known.

All of us have remnants of what Luther called the "old Adam" deep within us. There is a "dark side" that always seeks to press its way forward, extorting the joy and the light. In his typical humorous way, Luther one time quipped that, despite the fact God drowns the old

Adam in the waters of Baptism, Adam is a very good swimmer. There is One, however, who can wipe away the tears, extort the stubborn woe, and cheer the mournful heart, with love divine.

Pray

God of steadfast love, the words of Thomas often become our own: "Lord, we do not know where you are going. How can we know the way?" In those moments, open our eyes that we might see the Light surrounding us at all times, even the Christ, your Son. Amen.

SATURDAY IN LENT I

Read

To you, O Lord, I lift up my soul. . . . Make me to know your ways, O Lord; teach me your paths. Lead me in your truth, and teach me, for you are the God of my salvation; for you I wait all day long. Be mindful of your mercy, O Lord, and of your steadfast love, for they have been from of old. Do not remember the sins of my youth or my transgressions; according to your steadfast love remember me, for your goodness' sake, O Lord! . . . Turn to me and be gracious to me, for I am lonely and afflicted. Relieve the troubles of my heart, and bring me out of my distress. Consider my affliction and my trouble, and forgive all my sins. (Psalm 25:1, 4–7, 16–18)

Sing

Meter: 10 10.11.11

This hymn can be sung to "Lyons," the tune used for "How Firm a Foundation."

> My Jesus, my hope,
>   When will he appear
> A soul to lift up
>   That waits for him here,
> In much tribulation,
>   In trouble's excess,

In height of temptation,
    And depth of distress!

O when shall I see
    An end of my pain,
And triumph in thee
    My Savior again?
Lord, hasten the hour,
    Thy kingdom bring in,
And give me the power
    To live without sin.

Jesus, thou know'st
    My sorrowful load,
And seest that my trust
    Is all in thy blood:
Thou wilt have compassion,
    My burden remove,
Thy name is salvation,
    Thy nature is love.

Thy nature and name
    My portion shall be
Who humbly lay claim
    To all things in thee:
The days of my mourning
    And painful distress
Shall at thy returning
    Eternally cease.
        (*Redemption Hymns*, Hymn 36)

Reflect

This has been a difficult week. We have explored some of the situations in which we find ourselves crying to God, out of the depths. The posture of the Psalmist, alluded to in the opening sentence of the Psalm, characterizes our posture as we reach out to God. The most common gesture of prayer in ancient Israel, and still today, involves lifting up one's hands in a supplicating manner. The gesture itself expresses the fact that we hold *our lives* in hands outstretched to God, saying in effect that our lives depend completely and only on God. We entreat God to hear, to act, to forgive, to love us still. With the Psalmist, we know that God must teach us our path and lead us into the truth. Without God we remain in the darkness, lonely and afflicted. Wesley's alliteration in the first stanza of the hymn serves to intensify the tragic dimension of the state in which we find ourselves apart from God. Tribulation. Trouble's excess. The height of temptation. We long for an end to our pain, carry a "sorrowful load," languish in "painful distress." This is serious business. Wesley offers no easy panacea for our affliction, no simple solution, no power of positive thinking, no rose-colored, put-a-smile-on-your-face prescription for these woes. An absolute realism characterizes his portrayal of our situation as we have seen throughout the week. But while his *Redemption Hymns* paint a pessimistic picture of the human condition—a condition that cries out for a Redeemer—he never fails to point to his profound optimism in God's grace and love.

Weary and burdened, we cry to God out of the depths. We ask God to give us clean hearts and to turn our hearts of stone into hearts of flesh. Often lost and struggling in the darkness, we plead for God to help us find our way. Wesley's hymn directs our attention to the God of mercy, steadfast love, grace, and forgiveness to whom the Psalmist cries. He annunciates the central theme in the very first line: "My Jesus, my hope." Despite the tribulation and distress, we can live as those who have hope. In the second stanza, we find the ultimate answer in the question itself. The operative words are triumph and power. Jesus is the One who brings victory in the midst of our anguish. The pain will not last forever, for Jesus has already triumphed over evil and sin and offers the benefits of resurrection to us. He is the One who possesses the power to restore our ability to love as we have been loved by God. Jesus knows us. Jesus knows me fully. Realizing that we are fully known and fully loved by a compassionate God actually restores the latent capacity to "trust" in us all. Wesley concludes with the triumphant affirmation, expressed in similar words throughout his corpus: "Thy name is salvation. Thy nature is love." In the final stanza Wesley carries over this "nature/name" language, exclaiming, in effect, "thy nature and thy name is love—throughout eternity." No reality in the universe is more important than this.

Pray

O Lord, be mindful of your mercy, remember me according to your steadfast love, turn to me and be gracious to me, for I am lonely and afflicted. Consider my affliction and my trouble, and forgive all my sins, for the sake of Jesus Christ, whose nature and name is love. Amen.

Lent II: Friend of Sinners

The Second Sunday in Lent

Read

Jesus went out again beside the lake; the whole crowd gathered around him, and he taught them. As he was walking along, he saw Levi son of Alphaeus sitting at the tax booth, and he said to him, "follow me." And he got up and followed him. And as he sat at dinner in Levi's house, many tax-collectors and sinners were also sitting with Jesus and his disciples— for there were many who followed him. When the scribes of the Pharisees saw that he was eating with sinners and tax-collectors, they said to his disciples, "Why does he eat with tax-collectors and sinners?" When Jesus heard this, he said to them, "Those who are well have no need of a physician, but those who are sick; I have come to call not the righteous but sinners." (Mark 2:13–17)

Sing

Meter: SMD

This hymn can be sung to "St. Michael," the tune used for "O Day of God, Draw Nigh."

> Jesus, my Lord, attend
> Thy fallen creature's cry,
> And show thyself the sinner's friend,
> And set me up on high;
> From hell's oppressive power,
> From earth and sin release,
> And to thy Father's grace restore,
> And to thy perfect peace.
>
> For this, alas! I mourn,
> In helpless unbelief,
> But thou my wretched heart canst turn,
> And heal my sin and grief;

Salvation in thy name
To dying souls is given,
And all may, through thy merit, claim
A right to life and heaven.

Thy blood and righteousness
I make my only plea,
My present and eternal peace
Are both derived from thee;
Rivers of life divine
From thee their fountain flow,
And all who know that love of thine,
The joy of angels know.

O then impute, impart
To me thy righteousness,
And let me taste how good thou art,
How full of truth and grace:
That thou canst here forgive
I long to testify,
And justified by faith to live,
And in that faith to die.
(*Redemption Hymns*, Hymn 1)

Reflect

When I was a young pastor, I increased the frequency of the celebration of Holy Communion in the church to which I had recently been called. Several months into this changed pattern of worship I noticed that one woman in particular attended every week, but never participated in the Sacrament. I requested a meeting with her to find out why she abstained and to see if there was something I could do for her as her pastor to open the door to this means of grace. We talked for some time about life in general, and I eventually asked her directly about her reason for avoiding the table. She said that she did not feel worthy to accept Jesus' invitation to the meal. She felt that she was not good enough to be so close to Jesus in that way.

I gently drew her attention to the gospels and to the stories there about Jesus and meals. Our survey of those meal narratives included this account of Levi: Jesus calls. Levi the tax-collector follows. Jesus and his disciples end up eating with sinners in his home, and this chain of events throws the religious leaders into a tizzy. A respectable person simply would not act this way, would not associate with such people, would not accept hospitality and share time with persons who were obviously so far from God. I asked my friend, "Who did Jesus choose as his table companions? With whom did he long to eat?" The answer was obvious. Jesus ate with unworthy sinners. These were the people with whom he shared his bread, the ones he invited to be his "companions" in life. I tried to help my friend see that Jesus offers all of us that same invitation today. Rather than creating a barrier to fellowship at the meal, the fact of our brokenness qualifies us to sit at table with Jesus. He yearns to share his love and acceptance with us. He feeds us because we are hungry. He fills us because we are empty. He meets us at our point of need, and offers us a most precious gift at the table—his friendship.

One of Charles Wesley's favorite titles for Jesus is "Friend of Sinners." This week, we will encounter this image many times over. He introduces this image in the very first stanza of his *Redemption Hymns* collection. "Show thyself the sinner's friend," he pleads, and then projects where this friendship leads. When Jesus befriends us and we permit God's grace to open our hearts to him, that friendship liberates, and heals, and restores us. The dominant verbs of Wesley's hymn reflect his vision of redemption. Release. Forgive. Heal. Restore. Impute. Impart. Jesus—the sinner's friend—releases us from the oppressive power of evil and forgives our sin. Intimacy with this companion heals our wounds and restores the image of God in our lives. This friend not only offers us the gift of his own righteousness, but through the power of his Spirit enables us to actually become more and more like him in every way, if we but open our lives to his presence, peace, and power.

Pray

Friend of Sinners, help me to accept your invitation to be your companion throughout life: Feed me through Word and Sacrament, release me from all that binds my loving heart, and restore your glorious image in my life, for your love's sake. Amen.

MONDAY IN LENT II

Read

Those who have clean hands and pure hearts, who do not lift up their souls to what is false, and do not swear deceitfully, They will receive blessing from the Lord, and vindication from the God of their salvation. Such is the company of those who seek him, who seek the face of the God of Jacob. Selah Lift up your heads, O gates! and be lifted up, O ancient doors! that the King of glory may come in. Who is the King of glory? The Lord, strong and mighty, the Lord, mighty in battle. Lift up your heads, O gates! and be lifted up, O ancient doors! that the King of glory may come in. Who is this King of glory? The Lord of hosts, he is the King of glory. Selah. (Psalm 24:4–10)

Sing

Meter: 66.66.88

This hymn can be sung to "Gopsal," the tune used for "Rejoice, the Lord Is King."

You tempted souls, that feel
    The great and sore distress,
Waiting till Christ reveal
    His joy, and love, and peace;
Lift up your heads, the signs appear,
Look up, and see your Savior near!

Long have you heard and known
    The wars that rage within,
And nature still fights on,
    And grace opposes sin:
Lift up your heads, the signs appear,
Look up, and see your Savior near!

That plague of your own heart,
    Which poisons all the race,
Shall suddenly depart,
    Expelled by sovereign grace:
Lift up your heads, the signs appear,
Look up, and see your Savior near!

Who patiently endure,
    Till all these trials end,
Are of salvation sure,
    And shall to heaven ascend:
Lift up your heads, the signs appear,
Look up, and see your Savior here.
        (*Redemption Hymns*, Hymn 8.1–2, 5, 10)

Reflect

Who is this friend of sinners? He is the King of Glory! The repeated concluding couplet of Wesley's hymn echoes Psalm 24:

Lift up your heads, the signs appear,
Look up, and see your Savior near!

For all those who have ever heard—witnessed—George Friedrich Handel's *Messiah*, the potent cadences and resounding choral responses to the question "Who is this King of Glory?" immediately flood the memory. This famous chorus comes at the critical turning point in Part Two, the "redemption" portion of the oratorio. It is the strategic center of this great work. Strategic, powerful, and uplifting, Handel's chorus transports those who have followed the narrative like a burst of insight.

In the Psalm, entrance is demanded for the "King of Glory," a title that appears nowhere else in the Hebrew Testament. Glory belongs to this figure because he has proven himself to be a powerful warrior and ruler over all things. In the first response to the question concerning his identity, victory reveals his glorious reign. The second answer describes this King as "Lord of Hosts," the throne name of Israel's God. This is the One who protects Zion and its inhabitants and makes the city of God invulnerable. Under the protection of this Lord, all are safe; righteousness, justice, steadfast love, and faithfulness character- ize the reign of this Lord. This amazing entrance liturgy emphasizes two important aspects related to the King of Glory: He comes! He is faithful and victorious!

In the same way that Handel applies this text to Christ, so too Wesley transmutes the image into Christ's entrance into the human soul so that God's children might be temples of the Holy Spirit. Christ's presence in them is like that of the ark in the temple. It cleanses and purifies them. The first stanza of the hymn portrays those who await the arrival of the King. They are tossed about by temptation, anxi- ety, and distress. In the second stanza Wesley elaborates this inte- rior dimension in which grace wages war against nature. He implies that this interior battle requires a powerful warrior to root out sin. Faithlessness plagues the heart and can only be expelled by the sudden victory of grace. But those who persevere—who patiently endure— experience the victory of the coming King. Each stanza reinforces the point that even now he approaches and prepares to enter.

> Lift up your heads, the signs appear,
> Look up, and see your Savior near!

Jesus stands at the door of your heart and knocks. Open the gates, open the doors of your heart, and let him in. This is the gospel call— the invitation and demand—that we permit the King of Glory to rule in our hearts and lives. In order to welcome this Lord properly, we ask, Who is this King of Glory? We get to know him by immersing our- selves in the means of grace. We entrust our lives to him. We learn how to love him above all others. Who is this King of Glory? He is righ- teousness, justice, steadfast love, and faithfulness, and in his care, we are always safe. He longs to reveal his joy, and love, and peace to you.

Pray

King of Glory, we know that you take the initiative to come to us and that you are always faithful: Help us to lift up our heads so that we can see you and to open our hearts that you might come in and dwell with us forever. Amen.

TUESDAY IN LENT II

Read

If we say that we have no sin, we deceive ourselves, and the truth is not in us. If we confess our sins, he who is faithful and just will forgive us our sins and cleanse us from all unrighteousness. If we say that we have not sinned, we make him a liar, and his word is not in us. My little children, I am writing these things to you so that you may not sin. But if anyone does sin, we have an advocate with the Father, Jesus Christ the righteous; and he is the atoning sacrifice for our sins, and not for ours only but also for the sins of the whole world. (1 John 1:8–2:2)

Sing

Meter: 886.886

This hymn can be sung to "Magdalen College," the tune used for "We Sing of God, the Mighty Source."

> Help, Jesus, help against my foe,
> Pity on your captive show,
>   Entangled in the snare,
> The hellish snare of sin I lie;
> O cast not out my plaintive prayer,
>   But save me, or I die.
>
> With all my soul I seek your face,
> Give me your restoring grace:
>   My agony of fear,
> And guilt, and shame, and sorrow end;
> Appear, my Advocate, appear,
>   And show yourself my friend.
>
> O might I feel your blood applied,
> Nothing would I ask beside:
>   Your love alone be given,
> I every other good resign,

Of all you have in earth or heaven,
Let love alone be mine!
(*Redemption Hymns*, Hymn 37)

Reflect

Two phrases in Wesley's hymn capture our attention because of their parallel construction: the opening words, "Help, Jesus, help," and the subsequent prayer, "Appear, my Advocate, appear." The first cry is an acknowledgment; the second supplication is an appeal.

My theological mentor, Dr. Robert Cushman, emphasized the importance of acknowledgment in all of his teaching. Socrates, one of his great heroes, encapsulated his famous philosophy of life in two simple words: "know yourself." We begin to face life with seriousness and honesty, according to St. Augustine, when we acknowledge the fact that we stand perennially *coram deo*—before God. The first step toward health and wholeness in all programs of recovery is the acknowledgment of our brokenness, the confession that we have a problem and that we cannot fix it ourselves. The plaintiffs who cry out, "Help, Jesus, help," acknowledge that they are entangled in a snare from which they cannot extricate themselves. The Johannine author makes the point twice for emphasis. "If we say that we have no sin, we deceive ourselves, and the truth is not in us. . . . If we say that we have not sinned, we make him a liar, and his word is not in us." Only God's truth and God's word have the power to liberate. As we stand before God, confronted with the awesome majesty and holiness of the Creator, we immediately acknowledge our failures, our brokenness, our sin. Acknowledgment begins our restoration. For Wesley this is a matter of life and death.

The second stanza opens with an acknowledgment of the all-embracing nature of this quest: "With all my soul I seek your face." Agony characterizes the life of the sinner separated from God. Note the interior feelings Wesley piles up concerning this alienation: fear, guilt, shame, sorrow. Only God's grace can transform this depth of despair into peace, forgiveness, reconciliation, and joy. And so, the plaintiff appeals through a second prayer: "Appear, my Advocate, appear, and show yourself my friend." Truly, we all need such a friend. All of us need Someone to plead our cause, to come to our defense, to support us, and stand by us in our agony. We already know this Friend and Advocate.

His name is Jesus Christ the righteous. Not only does he befriend us, he himself "is the atoning sacrifice for our sins, and not for ours only but also for the sins of the whole world." When we fall short of God's loving intentions for us, he takes his place at our side. He enables us to find the right words and an authentic way to acknowledge our sin, but he also helps us to discover another fact about ourselves that we are called to acknowledge. He helps us to understand that despite our sin and brokenness, we are God's beloved children. He reveals who we are in the deepest part of ourselves. He atones for our sin, but he also embraces us as his brothers and sisters created in the image of God. He elicits from us that most sacred and fundamental aspect of our true identity. In the process of acknowledging our sin and discovering our true identity, we sing, in the end, "Let love alone be mine!"

Pray

Help, Jesus, help us, for we are entangled in a trap of self-deception and sin from which we cannot free ourselves; appear, Advocate, appear, and show yourself our friend, for we long for a true self-understanding that will open the way to peace and joy in our lives. Amen.

WEDNESDAY IN LENT II

Read

Not even the first covenant was inaugurated without blood. For when every commandment had been told to all the people by Moses in accordance with the law, he took the blood of calves and goats, with water and scarlet wool and hyssop, and sprinkled both the scroll itself and all the people, saying, "This is the blood of the covenant that God has ordained for you." And in the same way he sprinkled with the blood both the tent and all the vessels used in worship. Indeed, under the law almost everything is purified with blood, and without the shedding of blood there is no forgiveness of sins. . . . Therefore, my friends, since we have confidence to enter the sanctuary by the blood of Jesus, by the new and living way that he opened for us through the curtain (that is, through his flesh), and since we have a great priest over the house of God, let us approach with a true heart in full assurance of faith, with our hearts sprinkled clean from an evil conscience and our bodies washed with pure water. Let us hold fast to the confession of our hope without wavering, for he who has promised is faithful. (Hebrews 9:18–22, 10:19–23)

Sing
Meter: 77.77.77

This hymn can be sung to "Dix," the tune used for "Praise to God, Immortal Praise."

> Holy Lamb of God, to thee
> In my deep distress I flee,
> Thou didst purge my guilty stain,
> Didst for all atonement make;
> Take away my sin and pain,
> Save me for thy mercy's sake.

> Now thy mercy is my prop,
> And it bears my weakness up;
> Full of evil as I am,
> Fuller thou of pardoning grace,
> Jesus is thy healing name,
> Savior of the sinful race.

> For thine own dear sake, I pray,
> Take all now my sins away:
> Other refuge have I none,
> None do I desire beside;
> Thou hast died for all t'atone,
> Thou for me, for me hast died.

> Hast thou died that I might live,
> Might in thee my life receive;
> Hasten, Lord, my heart prepare,
> Bring thy death and sufferings in,
> Tear away my idols, tear,
> Save me, save me from my sin.

Bid it all from me depart
All this unbelief of heart,
All my mountain-sins remove,
Wrath, concupiscence, and pride,
Cast them out by perfect love,
Save me, who for me hast died.

This, O this is all my plea,
For thy blood was shed for me,
Shed, to wash my conscience clean,
Shed to purify my heart,
Shed to purge me from all sin,
Shed to make me as thou art.

Flood me with thy cleansing tide
Leave no space for sin to hide;
Plunge me in the crimson flood,
Drown my sins in the Red Sea,
Bring me now, e'en now to God,
Swallow up my soul in thee!
                              (*Redemption Hymns*, Hymn 24)

Reflect

The Letter to the Hebrews explores the image of sacrifice, both as a practice to reconnect the people to their covenant God in ancient Israel and as Christ's offering of himself on the cross in that great sacrifice of love. I will be honest and confess that the "blood" imagery of sacrifice has never affected me as deeply as it seems to move many. In some ways, it raises more questions in my mind than it provides satisfying answers to the perplexing questions of atonement and the ways in which God deals with sin. One insight that has helped me over the years relates to the concept of sacrifice in the Hebrew scriptures. Quite simply, blood represents life, not death. Wesley reflects this understanding in many of his hymns, especially those related to the Eucharist, where he talks about the blood of Christ being "poured into our hearts." The blood which Jesus shed is "blood of life" for me.

For me! The Wesley hymn for today is one of his most personal testimonies to the power of Christ's blood. In this hymn of forty-two lines, he employs the personal pronouns "me" and "my" no less than thirty times. On the negative side of the "atonement equation," he describes "my deep distress," "my guilty stain," "my sin and pain," "my weakness," "my sins," several times, "my idols," "my mountain-sins." The singer pleads four times for God to "save me." Repetition often emphasizes the personal dimension of this connection with God through Christ: "Save me, save me from my sin," "Save me, who for me hast died." Despite the chasm that separates us from God and God's intentions for us, Charles declares that God's pardoning grace is wider, fuller still. This grace, he emphasizes on at least two occasions in this hymn, God offers to all, for Jesus "didst for *all* atonement make." "Thou hast died for *all* t'atone." Love excludes none from this gift. As in all of Wesley's hymns, the verbs do the work and provide the power of his lyrical theology. Hasten. Purge. Tear away. And particularly in the closing stanza, the more mystical action to flood, plunge, drown, swallow up.

No verb serves his purposes more effectively, however, than the verb "to shed." Certainly, stanza six brings climax to the hymn as the Spirit of God applies the effects of Jesus' sacrifice on our behalf, his blood "shed for me." Wesley elevates four aspects of God's work in refashioning the soul. Christ's blood was shed "to wash my conscience clean." How liberating it is to be able to look God and others in the face! Christ's blood was shed "to purify my heart." How exhilarating it is to live with a clean spirit! Christ's blood was shed "to purge me from all sin." How empowering it is to have the burden of the past lifted! Christ's blood was shed "to make me as thou art." More important than anything else, for the Wesleys, the sacrifice of Christ restores our capacity to love as we have been loved by God. This is good news indeed!

Pray

Holy Lamb of God, flood us with your cleansing tide, plunge us into the center of your will and way, drown all those thoughts and actions that alienate us from you, and bring us to God where we can be immersed in love forever. Amen.

THURSDAY IN LENT II

Read

Beloved, let us love one another, because love is from God; everyone who loves is born of God and knows God. Whoever does not love does not know God, for God is love. God's love was revealed among us in this way: God sent his only Son into the world so that we might live through him. In this is love, not that we loved God but that he loved us and sent his Son to be the atoning sacrifice for our sins. Beloved, since God loved us so much, we also ought to love one another. No one has ever seen God; if we love one another, God lives in us, and his love is perfected in us. (1 John 4:7–12)

Sing

Meter: 87.87 D

This hymn can be sung to "Hyfrydol," the traditional setting for this hymn.

> Love divine, all loves excelling,
>> Joy of heaven to earth come down,
> Fix in us thy humble dwelling,
>> All thy faithful mercies crown;
> Jesu, thou art all compassion,
>> Pure unbounded love thou art,
> Visit us with thy salvation,
>> Enter every trembling heart.
>
> Breathe, O breathe thy loving Spirit
>> Into every troubled breast,
> Let us all in thee inherit,
>> Let us find that second rest:
> Take away our power of sinning,
>> Alpha and Omega be,
> End of faith as its beginning,
>> Set our hearts at liberty.
>
> Come, Almighty to deliver,
>> Let us all thy life receive,

Suddenly return, and never,
    Never more thy temples leave.
Thee we would be always blessing,
    Serve thee as thy hosts above,
Pray, and praise thee without ceasing,
    Glory in thy perfect love.

Finish then thy new creation,
    Pure and sinless let us be,
Let us see thy great salvation,
    Perfectly restored in thee;
Changed from glory into glory,
    Till in heaven we take our place,
Till we cast our crowns before thee,
    Lost in wonder, love, and praise!
                    (*Redemption Hymns*, Hymn 9)

Reflect

Our hymn from yesterday ended with the prayer: "Swallow up my soul in thee!" The most famous of Wesley's *Redemption Hymns*, "Love Divine, All Loves Excelling," provides a profound exposition of this theme. You undoubtedly know it well and have sung it often. The Friend of Sinners—who is also the King of Glory, our Advocate, and the Victim/Victor who sheds his blood for us—embodies God's love. He puts flesh on what, for many, is an abstract idea. He transforms a noun into an action verb. Jesus incarnates the love of God in which all genuine love begins and ends. It would not be improper to say that, for Charles Wesley, life in Christ means to be swallowed up in the immensity of this love. The writer of First John makes the same point. In six verses he uses a form of the word "love" fifteen times. The grandeur of his insight and the majesty with which he develops the interwoven themes of God's love and our response to it by means of intense, loving (ethical) concern for others mitigate against all forms of sentimentality and shallowness. Wesley elevates us to the same heights in this eloquent and compelling prayer for a love-filled life.

First, Wesley acknowledges God as the source of pure, unbounded, extravagant love. This love walks into human history in the person of Jesus Christ. In him we see what genuine love looks like and how it behaves. Compassion defines God's life in the flesh.

Wesley binds the image of the One who "suffers with" us in the first stanza to the universal quest of "every troubled breast" in the second. Our hearts are restless, claimed Augustine, until they find their rest in God. Wesley never deviates from a vision of liberation and redemption for all. Notice the plural, therefore, rather than singular, constructions in Wesley's hymn from beginning to end. We are *all* troubled, but in Christ *all* can find rest. In Wesley's original, God not only takes away "our bent to sinning," a typical modern rendition, but removes the "power of sinning," a force displaced by the capacity to love.

In stanza three, he elaborates this theme. Having expelled this power, the Spirit fills the believer with the fullness of God. The second line can be read actually in two different ways, perhaps an intended double *entendre*. "Let us all" expresses the possibility of universal redemption, while "all thy life" implies God's desire to make us totally Christ-like, namely, as those in whom "all the fullness of God is pleased to dwell." Those conformed to the image of Christ in this life, claims Wesley, can be identified by their service, prayer, and praise.

In the final stanza the singer prays for God to continue this process of restoration, moving us closer and closer to maturity in Christ. Wesley defines this metamorphosis by the little word "till." We live in that time between what has been (what is no longer) and what will be (but is not yet). In this meantime, God continues to change us from one degree of glory to another, conforming us to the image of Christ, and sinking us deeper and deeper into love.

Pray

Love Divine, fix in us your humble dwelling, breathe your loving Spirit into our troubled breast, deliver us from all that impedes our growth in grace, and finish the work you have begun in us that we might be lost in wonder, love and praise. Amen.

FRIDAY IN LENT II

Read

The voice of my beloved! Look, he comes, leaping upon the mountains, bounding over the hills. My beloved is like a gazelle or a young stag. Look, there he stands behind our wall, gazing in at the windows, looking through the lattice. My beloved speaks and says to me: "Arise, my love, my fair one, and come away; for now the winter is past, the rain is over and gone. The flowers appear on the earth; the time of singing has come, and the voice of the turtle dove is heard in our land. The fig tree puts forth its figs, and the vines are in blossom; they give forth fragrance. Arise, my love, my fair one, and come away." (Song of Songs 2:8–13)

Sing

Meter: 88.88.88

This hymn can be sung to "St. Catherine," the tune used for "Faith of Our Fathers."

> Jesu, as taught by thee, I pray,
>> Preserve me till I see thy light,
> Still let me for thy coming stay,
>> Stop a poor wavering sinner's flight,
> Till thou my full Redeemer art,
>> O keep, in mercy keep my heart.
>
> Keep, till this icy state is past,
>> This wintry state of doubts and fears,
> Exposed to passion's fiercest blast,
>> With horrors chilled, and drowned in tears,
> Bound up in sin and grief I mourn,
>> And languish for the spring's return.
>
> O might I hear the turtle's voice,
>> The cooing of thy gentle dove,
> The call that bids my heart rejoice,
>> "Arise, and come away my love,
> The storm is gone, the winter's o'er,
>> Arise, for thou shalt weep no more."
>
> When shall this shadowy Sabbath end,
>> This tedious length of legal woe?
> O would my Lord the substance send!

O might I now his rising know!
Come, Lord, and chase the clouds away,
        And bring thine own auspicious day.

Give me to bow with thee my head,
        And sink into thy silent grave,
To rest among thy quiet dead,
        Till thou display thy power to save,
Thy resurrection's power exert,
        And rise triumphant in my heart.
                    (*Redemption Hymns*, Hymn 28)

Reflect

I sang this text from Song of Songs before I ever read it. I think that was a proper way to encounter this word. The love we encounter in Jesus woos us, revealing the same kind of magnetic attraction that draws the lover to her beloved.

The biblical poet draws imagery from the world of nature. The word-pictures energize the text. The beloved comes "leaping upon the mountains, bounding over the hills." The young stag stands majestically on the crest of the hill, noble, strong, his gaze fixed on the object of his love. The lover addresses his beloved: "The winter is past. The rain is over and gone. The flowers appear on the earth. The time of singing has come. The voice of the turtle-dove is heard in our land." The rhythmic cadence of the words draws us out and invites us into the joy. "Arise, my love, my fair one, and come away." Who would not go? Winter gives way to spring. Green buds appear on the stark limbs of the trees and the delicate shafts of the vine. The smell of the season fills the air. I am reminded of the scene in C. S. Lewis's classic tale *The Lion, the Witch, and the Wardrobe* when the spell of the White Witch has been broken and the ice and snow of the long winter in Narnia begin to melt away, replaced by the fresh, clean dawn of a renewed earth.

In his hymn, Charles Wesley exploits the same imagery, but develops an allegorical vision, like Lewis's, in which winter symbolizes the cold and icy state of existence apart from God and spring heralds new creation in Christ. He plays with and expands all the imagery of the beloved's song. The opening stanza simply alerts us to a coming, holding us in place, listening intently, as it were, for the voice of the beloved. Stanza two fixes our attention on the conditions of the soul in its wintery state. Doubts and fears petrify the soul. The fierce blast of passions takes away one's breath. Horrors chill and tears, like the rains of the season, drown the languishing soul.

Stanza three simply paraphrases the appeal of the beloved, a call, says Wesley, "that bids my heart rejoice."

> "Arise, and come away my love,
> The storm is gone, the winter's o'er,
> Arise, for thou shalt weep no more."

In this stanza and the one that precedes it, Wesley likens the winter rains to the tears of those who seek for new birth into a life of peace and joy. Whereas the poet develops all of these images with the season-cycle of England in mind, the original setting of the Song of Songs, of course, envisages something a little different. "Winter" referred most certainly to the "rainy season," something we experienced in the context of equatorial Africa, at the end of which the growing season starts in earnest. The turtle-dove, a migratory bird in Palestine, signaled the coming of the long-sought spring with a song. Come away. The winter is over and gone.

Pray

Beloved Friend, we sometimes feel trapped in the dismal season of winter in our lives, longing for the fresh air, the song of returning birds, and the fragrant smells of spring: Keep, in mercy keep our hearts, till this icy state is past. Amen.

Saturday in Lent II

Read

Let the same mind be in you that was in Christ Jesus, who, though he was in the form of God, did not regard equality with God as something to be exploited, but emptied himself, taking the form of a slave, being born in human likeness. And being found in human form, he humbled himself

and became obedient to the point of death—even death on a
cross. Therefore God also highly exalted him and gave him
the name that is above every name, so that at the name of Jesus
every knee should bend, in heaven and on earth and under
the earth, and every tongue should confess that Jesus Christ is
Lord, to the glory of God the Father. (Philippians 2:5–11)

Sing

Meter: CMD

This hymn can be sung to "The Third Tune," the tune used for
"To Mock Your Reign, O Dearest Lord."

> Jesus, my strength and righteousness,
>   My Savior and my King,
> Triumphantly your name I bless,
>   Your conquering name I sing.
> You, Lord, have magnified your name,
>   You have maintained your cause,
> And I enjoy the glorious shame,
>   The scandal of your cross.
>
> The name inscribed in the white stone,
>   The unbeginning Word,
> The mystery so long unknown,
>   The secret of the Lord;
> The living bread sent down from heaven,
>   The saints' and angels' food,
> Th'immortal seed, the little leaven,
>   The effluence of God!
>
> The tree of life that blooms and grows
>   In th' midst of paradise,
> The pure and living stream, that flows
>   Back to its native skies:
> The Spirit's law, the cov'nant's seal,
>   Th'eternal righteousness,
> The glorious joy unspeakable,
>   Th'unutterable peace!

The treasure in the gospel field,
    The wisdom from above,
Hid from the wise, to babes revealed,
    The precious pearl of love;
The mystic power of godliness,
    The end of death and sin,
The antepast of heavenly bliss,
    The kingdom fixed within.

The Morning Star, that glittering bright,
    Shines to the perfect day,
The Sun of Righteousness. The light,
    The life, the truth, the way:
The image of the living God,
    His nature, and his mind,
Himself he hath on us bestowed,
    And all in Christ we find.
        (*Redemption Hymns*, Hymn 17.1, 6–9)

Reflect

Philippians 2:5–11 is one of those great epicenters of the Christian Testament. Many scholars believe that St. Paul draws this statement about the humiliation and exaltation of Christ from one of the earliest hymns of the church. Christians in the first century sang these words to confess their faith in the one who humbled himself, became obedient to death on a cross for us, and now sits on the throne of God for all to worship and adore. Wesley reformulates this early confession for the purpose of actually singing it in the first stanza of a hymn that celebrates the names of Jesus. He reverses the order of the original text, proclaiming first the strength and righteousness of the Savior and King who, having triumphed over death and sin, now receives the blessing of all. We praise his name because we now are the beneficiaries of the scandal of the cross. Just as God has magnified the name of Jesus, so Wesley elevates the many names of this One who came to save and restore all of God's children. Instead of providing a brief meditation on these various names for your reflection, it might be more valuable simply to let you ponder the significance of each in turn. Take time to consider the various terms or names associated with Christ. I have provided references for scriptural allusions for you to explore them in their original context if you wish. Blessed be the name of the Lord.

> The unbeginning Word (John 1:1)
> The mystery so long unknown (Ephesians 3:9)
> The living bread (John 6:51)
> The immortal seed (2 Timothy 2:8)
> The little leaven (Galatians 5:9)
> The effluence of God (Colossians 1:19)
> The tree of life (Revelation 22:2)
> The pure and living stream (Zechariah 13:1)
> The Spirit's law (Romans 8:2)
> The covenant's seal (Genesis 17:11)
> The eternal righteousness (Psalm 119:142)
> The glorious joy unspeakable (1 Peter 1:8)
> The unutterable peace (Philippians 4:7)
> The treasure in the gospel field (Matthew 13:44)
> The wisdom from above (Proverbs 8:12)
> The precious pearl of love (Matthew 13:45–46)
> The mystic power of godliness (2 Timothy 3:5)
> The end of death and sin (Romans 8:2)
> The antepast of heavenly bliss (Hebrews 6:4–5)
> The kingdom fixed within (Luke 17:20–21)
> The Morning Star (Revelation 22:16)
> The Sun of Righteousness (Malachi 4:2)
> The light (John 8:12)
> The life (Colossians 3:4)
> The truth (John 14:6)
> The way (John 14:6)
> The image of the living God (2 Corinthians 4:4)

Pray

Jesus, you are the King of Glory, the eternal Son of the Father; you humbly accepted the Virgin's womb, overcame the sting of death, and opened the kingdom of heaven to all believers. You are seated at God's right hand in glory. We adore you; we bless you; we praise your name. Amen.

LENT III: GROANING FOR REDEMPTION

THE THIRD SUNDAY IN LENT

Read

My God, my God, why have you forsaken me? Why are you so far from helping me, from the words of my groaning? O my God, I cry by day, but you do not answer; and by night, but find no rest. Yet you are holy, enthroned on the praises of Israel. In you our ancestors trusted; they trusted, and you delivered them. To you they cried, and were saved; in you they trusted, and were not put to shame. (Psalm 22:1–5)

Sing

Meter: CMD

This hymn can be sung to "Halifax," the tune used for "And Have the Bright Immensities."

> Thou hidden God, for whom I groan,
> Till thou thyself declare,
> God inaccessible, unknown,
> Regard a sinner's prayer;
> A sinner weltering in his blood,
> Unpurged and unforgiven,
> Far distant from the living God,
> As far as hell from heaven.
>
> An unregenerate child of man
> On thee for faith I call,
> Pity thy fallen creature's pain,
> And raise me from my fall.
> The darkness which through thee I feel
> Thou only canst remove,
> Thine own eternal power reveal,
> Thy deity of love.

Thou hast in unbelief shut up,
    That grace may let me go:
In hope believing against hope,
    I wait the truth to know.
Thou wilt in me reveal thy name,
    Thou wilt thy light afford:
Bound, and oppressed, yet thine I am,
    The prisoner of the Lord.

I would not to thy foe submit,
    But hate the tyrant's chain:
Send forth thy prisoner from the pit,
    Nor let me cry in vain:
Show me the blood that bought my peace,
    The covenant blood apply,
And all my griefs at once shall cease,
    And all my sins shall die.

Now, Lord, if thou art power, descend,
    The mountain-sin remove,
My unbelief and troubles end,
    If thou art truth and love:
Speak, Jesu, speak into my heart
    What thou for me hast done,
One grain of living faith impart,
    And God is all my own.
        (*Redemption Hymns*, Hymn 27)

Reflect

The Wesley brothers entitled one of the major sections in their monumental 1780 *Collection of Hymns*, "Groaning for Full Redemption." They did not carelessly jumble their hymns together, but ordered them on the basis of the experience of real Christians. Not only did Charles compose hymns for believers rejoicing, fighting, praying, watching, and working, he also acknowledged the fact that believers groan. We groan, in fact, from the deepest part of our being. Through groans, the heart cries out to God. References to groaning do not abound in the Bible, but when they do occur they signal something extremely important. Groaning often precedes important breakthroughs or victories. Perhaps this is why the Apostle Paul links groaning with a mother's experience of childbirth. The whole creation groans in anticipation of the marvelous work of God. Groaning precedes redemption. Groaning anticipates new birth, new life, new creation.

These groans often express the distress we feel when in pain and separated from those we love. When we are caught up in situations we cannot understand or alienated from the source of our joy and peace in life, all we can do is groan. These groans express our deep need for reconciliation, connectedness, and communion. And let us not forget that God groans. That is probably a rather foreign thought for you, but in the person of Jesus Christ, God lives in solidarity with us in our groaning. Jesus experienced the same depth of alienation and separation that sometimes characterizes our lives, and he shares our groaning. In the midst of his agony on the cross, Jesus quoted Psalm 22, confirming for all time the depth of his solidarity with all who experience alienation, separation, and long so deeply for communion with God. "My God, my God, why have you forsaken me?" he cried with the Psalmist. "Why are you so far from helping me, from the words of my groaning?" When Martin Luther was lecturing on the Psalms at the University of Wittenberg, and came upon these words, the concept of a judgmental God that had long dominated his thinking began to change. He described Jesus thereafter as "the derelict on the cross" who truly understood his own groans. The blending of Jesus' groans with his own signaled a major transformation that the Spirit was working in his soul.

Charles Wesley's hymn expresses the same depth of distress to which Jesus bore witness on the cross—that abysmal feeling of separation from God. The God to whom we groan is hidden, inaccessible, unknown. Sometimes we feel so far from God that the chasm seems as wide as that which separates heaven from hell. Our own groaning echoes in our ears, but we yearn to hear another voice. We hope against hope that our groaning precedes a new word, a message of truth and love. "Speak into my heart, Jesus," we pray. "Tell me what you have done for me. Plant one tiny grain of living faith in my soul, and God is all my own." "To you they cried," exclaims the Psalmist, "and were saved."

Pray

Attentive God, sometimes I feel so far from you and that feeling of separation and alienation breaks my heart; accept my groans as a heartfelt plea for forgiveness and reconciliation, for I yearn to be close to you again. Amen.

MONDAY IN LENT III

Read

"The kingdom of heaven is like treasure hidden in a field, which someone found and hid; then in his joy he goes and sells all that he has and buys that field. Again, the kingdom of heaven is like a merchant in search of fine pearls; on finding one pearl of great value, he went and sold all that he had and bought it." (Matthew 13:44–46)

Sing

Meter: 10.11.10.11

This hymn can be sung to "Paderborn," the tune used for "Ye Servants of God."

> Come, Lord, from above,
> The mountains remove,
> Overturn all that hinders the course of thy love;
> My bosom inspire,
> Enkindle the fire,
> And wrap my whole soul in the flames of desire:
>
> I languish and pine
> For the comfort divine:
> O when shall I say, my beloved is mine!
> I have chose the good part,
> My portion thou art,
> O love, I have found thee, O God, in my heart!
>
> For this my heart sighs,
> Nothing else can suffice:

How, Lord, shall I purchase the pearl of great price?
   It cannot be bought:
   And thou know'st I have nought,
Not an action, a word, or a truly good thought.

   But I hear a voice say,
   Without money you may
Receive it, whoever have nothing to pay:
   Who on Jesus relies,
   Without money or price
The pearl of forgiveness and holiness buys.

   The blessing is free:
   So, Lord, let it be;
I yield that thy love should be given to me.
   I freely receive
   What thou freely dost give,
And consent in thy love, in thy Eden, to live.

   The gift I embrace,
   The Giver I praise,
And ascribe my salvation to Jesus' grace:
   It comes from above,
   The foretaste I prove,
And I soon shall receive all thy fullness of love.
                    (*Redemption Hymns*, Hymn 5)

Reflect

When Philip Jakob Spener began his work to renew the church of his own day, he entitled his manifesto of reform *Pia Desideria*, a Latin phrase that can be translated as "heartfelt desire." He understood that nothing happens without desire, and that desire has to come from within. It has to be generated from what Howard Thurman described as the citadel of all my desiring—the heart. The word "desire" itself actually comes from a root related to the "heavenly bodies." To desire means to yearn for, to reach up to the heavens. Little wonder that when Charles Wesley reflects on the human quest for redemption, he prays to God on behalf of all to "wrap my whole soul in the flames of desire."

The galloping rhythm of Wesley's hymn (an adapted 5.5.12D) accentuates the desire for redemption in Christ. This passionate quest is like a flame that races about (like the hymn) to consume all lesser desires in its path. Without God we languish and pine—as we have seen, we groan—for God's comforting presence in our lives. Nothing but God will suffice. We yearn for the pearl of great price as if nothing else matters in life. Wesley develops this well-known theme unique to Matthew's Gospel in several stanzas.

The merchant sells all that he has in order to obtain the most special of pearls. But the story takes a different twist in the hands of Wesley. He turns the image of purchase on its head as he relates the quest for redemption to the wonder of God's grace. In his hymn, the pearl remains beyond the reach of the one who yearns for it because no action, word, or thought can purchase it. But with regard to forgiveness and holiness—Wesley's interpretation of the essence of the pearl—God requires no capital of our own to secure this great treasure in our lives. "Without money you may receive it, whoever have nothing to pay." For those with heartfelt desire, who yearn for these things with their whole heart, God only requires that they rely on Jesus—that they put their whole trust and confidence in him. The short lines of the two concluding stanzas punctuate the wonder of God's grace: the blessing is free; I freely receive; the gift I embrace; the Giver I praise. The long lines enunciate the profound personal dimension of this amazing gift, the foundation of which Wesley articulated earlier in the hymn: "O love, I have found thee, O God, in my heart!" "I yield that thy love should be given to me." "And consent in thy love, in thy Eden, to live."

Early in his collection of hymns on the theme of redemption, Wesley emphasizes two central themes in his vision of the Christian life. First, heartfelt desire for God—groaning, yearning, longing for communion with our Creator—defines the source and goal of our lives. Second, God reaches out to us long before we "reach up to the heavens" and offers us the most precious of gifts—grace. This pearl of great price is a free gift for all and in all.

Pray

Gracious Lord, we yearn with a heartfelt desire for your grace, mercy, forgiveness, and love, knowing that these are the gifts you offer to each and every one of us through Jesus Christ, our Lord and our Redeemer. Amen.

TUESDAY IN LENT III

Read

As they were leaving Jericho, a large crowd followed him. There were two blind men sitting by the roadside. When they heard that Jesus was passing by, they shouted, "Lord, have mercy on us, Son of David!" The crowd sternly ordered them to be quiet; but they shouted even more loudly, "Have mercy on us, Lord, Son of David!" Jesus stood still and called them, saying, "What do you want me to do for you?" They said to him, "Lord, let our eyes be opened." Moved with compassion, Jesus touched their eyes. Immediately they regained their sight and followed him. (Matthew 20:29–34)

Sing

Meter: 77.77

This hymn can be sung to "The Call," the tune used for "Come, My Way, My Truth, My Life."

> Depth of mercy! Can there be
> Mercy still reserved for me!
> Can my God his wrath forbear,
> Me, the chief of sinners spare!
>
> I have long withstood his grace,
> Long provoked him to his face,
> Would not hearken to his calls,
> Grieved him by a thousand falls.
>
> I my Master have denied,
> I afresh have crucified,
> Oft profaned his hallowed name,
> Put him to an open shame.

There for me the Savior stands,
Shows his wounds, and spreads his hands,
God is love: I know, I feel,
Jesus weeps! But loves me still!

If I rightly read thy heart,
If thou all compassion art,
Bow thine ear, in mercy bow,
Pardon, and accept me now.

Pity from thine eye let fall;
By a look my soul recall,
Now the stone to flesh convert,
Cast a look, and break my heart.

Now incline me to repent,
Let me now my fall lament;
Now my foul revolt deplore,
Weep, believe, and sin no more!

(*Hymns and Sacred Poems* [1740],
pp. 82–84, vv. 1–3, 9, 11–13)

Reflect

God's grace takes our breath away; God's mercy fills us with the breath of life. Grace and mercy are the twin anchors of redemption. Both are rooted in the compassionate character of the God we have seen in the life and ministry of Jesus. Jesus heals two blind men, and the story of this miracle revolves around the simple statement, "Moved with compassion, Jesus touched their eyes."

In one of Wesley's more familiar hymns, "Depth of Mercy," he plumbs the depths of this great mystery concerning God's nature, celebrated throughout the narrative of both Testaments and supremely manifest in the person of Jesus. Published originally in thirteen stanzas in the 1740 collection of *Hymns and Sacred Poems* (hereafter referred to as *HSP*), this hymn celebrates the nature of the One "whose property always is to have mercy." Many forces in life oppose our desire for God, but none is more devastating than sin. Charles Wesley understood the struggle against sin, even for the believer. But he also had confidence in the God of mercy who picks us up and sustains us in our journey toward our goal to "perfectly love God and worthily magnify God's holy name."

Wesley's hymn begins with deep, soul-searching questions. From God's great storehouse of compassion, can there be mercy still reserved for me? The second question intensifies the inquiry: "Can my God his wrath forbear, me, the chief of sinners spare!" With the blind men face to face with the Son of David, we can only cry, "*Kyrie eleison.*" Thomas Cranmer found the right words to express the predicament of all God's children and helped the faithful to express the deepest desire of their hearts:

We acknowledge and bewail our manifold sins and wickedness, which we from time to time most grievously have committed, by thought, word, and deed, against thy divine majesty. We do earnestly repent, and are heartily sorry for these our misdoings; the remembrance of them is grievous to us. Have mercy upon us, have mercy upon us, most merciful Father.

The second and third stanzas of Wesley's hymn stress the importance of this confession. The fact of the matter is that we often *withstand* God's grace, actually *provoke* God, *close* our ears to God's call, and *grieve* God "by a thousand falls." We *deny* Christ, *crucify* him anew, *profane* his name, and *shame* him by our words and actions. Stanza nine functions as a hinge upon which the miracle of transformation turns in this hymn. It is one of the most potent statements that Charles Wesley ever penned concerning God and God's relationship to us.

There for me the Savior stands,
Shows his wounds, and spreads his hands,
God is love: I know, I feel,
Jesus weeps! But loves me still!

Our sin is strong, but God's mercy is stronger still. When we allow ourselves to fall into the embrace of the compassionate Christ, we both *know* and *feel* God's love. Moreover, having experienced this mercy over and over again in our lives, we realize that we are called, not simply to be forgiven sinners, but to "weep, believe, and sin no more." We long to be more and more like Christ in every way.

Pray

Have mercy upon us, have mercy upon us, most merciful Father, for we have withstood, provoked, denied you, and crucified you in our hearts: Help us to fall into the embrace of Christ that we might know and feel your love. Amen.

WEDNESDAY IN LENT III

Read

Now faith is the assurance of things hoped for, the conviction of things not seen. Indeed, by faith our ancestors received approval. By faith we understand that the worlds were prepared by the word of God, so that what is seen was made from things that are not visible. . . . Therefore, since we are surrounded by so great a cloud of witnesses, let us also lay aside every weight and the sin that clings so closely, and let us run with perseverance the race that is set before us, looking to Jesus the pioneer and perfecter of our faith, who for the sake of the joy that was set before him endured the cross, disregarding its shame, and has taken his seat at the right hand of the throne of God. Consider him who endured such hostility against himself from sinners, so that you may not grow weary or lose heart. (Hebrews 11:1–3; 12:1–3)

Sing

Meter: LM

This hymn can be sung to "Old 100th," the tune used for "All People That on Earth Do Dwell."

> Author of faith, eternal word,
> > Whose Spirit breathes the active flame,
> Faith, like its Finisher and Lord,
> > Today, as yesterday the same;

To thee our humble hearts aspire,
    And ask the gift unspeakable:
Increase in us the kindled fire,
    In us the work of faith fulfill.

By faith we know thee strong to save,
    (Save us, a present Savior thou!)
Whate'er we hope, by faith we have,
    Future and past subsisting now.

To him that in thy name believes,
    Eternal life with thee is given,
Into himself he all receives,
    Pardon, and happiness, and heaven.

The things unknown to feeble sense,
    Unseen by reason's glimmering ray,
With strong, commanding evidence
    Their heavenly origin display.

Faith lends its realizing light,
    The clouds disperse, the shadows fly,
Th'invisible appears in sight,
    And God is seen by mortal eye.
                (*HSP* [1740], pp. 6–7)

Reflect

In a number of his hymns, Charles Wesley describes faith as "the gift unspeakable." He preached, wrote, and sang about faith. It is not too much to say that Christian faith defined his life and ministry. In his hymn on the "Author of faith," he describes the origins and nature of faith. He affirms the fact that faith is a gift, something related to the burning presence of the Spirit in the lives of the faithful. It is a source of knowledge concerning God and the way in which God offers salvation, hope, and healing to humanity. Faith illumines the child of God and enables spiritual vision. Like so many great Christian teachers, Wesley links the gift of faith to the capacity to trust God.

As a priest of the Church of England, Wesley frequently defended the conception of "true and lively faith" articulated by his church in the Anglican *Articles of Religion*. The English reformer and author of the *Book of Common Prayer*, Thomas Cranmer, embedded the same dynamic conception of faith in his *Homilies*, a rich theological reservoir in which Charles immersed himself and upon which he drew repeatedly as a source for his sermons and hymns. Like Cranmer, Wesley distinguished between "dead" and "living" faith. Faith is not simply what we say we believe, it is the dynamic foundation of our relationship with God. Like the definition provided in the Letter to the Hebrews, Wesley understood living faith to be a sure *trust* and *confidence* in the mercy and steadfast love of God. Whether described as the "experience of faith," "faith of the gospel," "spirit of faith," or simply "faith"—various expressions found throughout Wesley's writings—all connote the experience of having been accepted and pardoned by God through faith in Christ alone. The foundation of this concept, of course, is trust (*fiducia*). Faith is the gift of trust; the Spirit enabling us to entrust our lives into God's loving care.

"Faith"—a shorthand term for the theological concept is justification by grace through faith, therefore, is the door through which we pass into a vital relationship with God through Christ. I will never forget an encounter I had with a church member at the conclusion of a Lenten Bible study. She simply confessed: "I always had trouble understanding that business about salvation by faith. But once I experienced salvation as a gift, everything seemed clear and new." God offers that transforming discovery to all people all the time. The "act of faith," that living faith *by which* we believe is the doorway into a whole new world of hope and light. Within the worshiping community we receive and transmit this faith.

Ephesians 2:8 encapsulates Wesley's essential discovery concerning the Christian life: "for by grace you have been saved through faith; and this is not your own doing, it is the gift of God." Once we put our trust in God—once we accept God's unconditional love offered freely to us in Christ—then we begin to love God, others, and ourselves.

Pray

God of Grace and God of Glory, fill me in such a way with your Spirit that I will be able to put my whole trust and confidence in you; only in your hands am I safe and free to be your loving child. Amen.

THURSDAY IN LENT III

Read

For by grace you have been saved through faith, and this is not your own doing; it is the gift of God—not the result of works, so that no one may boast. For we are what he has made us, created in Christ Jesus for good works, which God prepared beforehand to be our way of life. (Ephesians 2:8–10)

Sing

Meter: 77.77

This hymn can be sung to "Savannah," the tune used for "Love's Redeeming Work Is Done."

> Let us plead for faith alone,
> Faith which by our works is shown;
> God it is who justifies,
> Only faith the grace applies,
>
> Active faith that lives within,
> Conquers hell, and death, and sin,
> Hallows whom it first made whole,
> Forms the Savior in the soul.
>
> Let us for this faith contend,
> Sure salvation, is its end;
> Heaven already is begun,
> Everlasting life is won:
>
> Only let us persevere
> Till we see our Lord appear,
> Never from the Rock remove,
> Saved by faith which works by love.
>
> (HSP [1740], p. 184, vv. 3–4)

Reflect

The very last line of the hymn provides a guideline for understanding Charles Wesley's entire vision of the Christian life: "Saved by faith which works by love." In this hymn, he demonstrates that the doctrine of salvation by faith is the only proper foundation upon which to build a life with God. In other words, faith is the essential response to God's prior offer of unconditional, loving relationship. But secondly, he maintains that the purpose of a life reclaimed by faith alone is the restoration of God's image, namely, love, in the life of the believer. In other words, holiness of heart and life is the goal toward which the Christian life moves, having been founded on faith. Faith is a means to love's end. Faith working by love leading to holiness of heart and life is the very essence of the gospel proclamation of free grace. Faith without activated love, on the one hand, and works founded upon anything other than God's grace, on the other, are equally deficient visions of the Christian life.

The biblical locus for this critical theme for both Wesley brothers is Galatians 5:6, "The only thing that counts is faith working through love." But even the classic "faith alone" text from the Letter to the Ephesians articulates the same vision: "For we are what he has made us, created in Christ Jesus for good works, which God prepared beforehand to be our way of life" (2:10). God calls us to faith-founded lives characterized by active goodness and love. While Charles Wesley's doctrine of salvation affirms the importance of justification by faith, it emphasizes the restorative process of salvation, the goal of which is the fullest possible love of God and neighbor.

Wesley's poetic reflections on Ephesians 2:8–10 provide the most memorable lyrical expression of this central theme. Note that this hymn is not a prayer, like most of his texts. Rather, Wesley exhorts and encourages the faithful to "plead for faith alone." The first two stanzas describe this faith. Despite the fact that Wesley always views God as the primary actor in this drama of redemption, faith is not passive, but active and ultimately serves to "form the Savior in the soul." The presence of Christ indwelling our lives shapes us, hopefully, in every possible way so that we are conformed increasingly to the full stature, the image of Christ. Since love is God's essence, through the power of the Spirit working within us God's love can become the very essence of our being as well. The hymn describes faith as an ongoing, life-transforming experience, something for which the child of God yearns and stretches forward to receive as a gift.

One other aspect of this vision is noteworthy. The journey toward the fullest possible love of God and neighbor, as Charles describes it in the hymn, requires a community of faithful companions. We sing in the plural, not the singular! It takes a fellowship of believers, shaped by God's grace, to teach the children of God how to love. The faithful persevere together toward the fruition of all loves in Christ.

Pray

Perfect God of Love, instill in us a vision of faith working by love leading to holiness of heart and life; teach us within the community of faith how to love you and all you have created in the same way that we have been loved by Christ, in whose name we pray. Amen.

Friday in Lent III

Read

For the love of Christ urges us on, because we are convinced that one has died for all; therefore all have died. And he died for all, so that those who live might live no longer for themselves, but for him who died and was raised for them. From now on, therefore, we regard no one from a human point of view; even though we once knew Christ from a human point of view, we know him no longer in that way. So if anyone is in Christ, there is a new creation: everything old has passed away; see, everything has become new! All this is from God, who reconciled us to himself through Christ, and has given us the ministry of reconciliation; that is, in Christ God was reconciling the world to himself, not counting their trespasses against them, and entrusting the message of reconciliation to us. So we are ambassadors for Christ, since God is making his appeal through us; we entreat you on behalf of Christ, be reconciled to God. For our sake he made him to be sin who knew no sin, so that in him we might become the righteousness of God. (2 Corinthians 5:14–21)

Sing

Meter: 88.88.88

This hymn can be sung to "Surrey," the tune used for "Creator Spirit, by Whose Aid."

Father of Jesus Christ the just,
    My friend and Advocate with thee,
Pity a soul, who fain would trust
    In him, who loved, and died for me;
But only thou canst make him known,
And in my heart reveal thy Son.

If drawn by thine alluring grace,
    My want of living faith I feel,
Show me in Christ thy smiling face;
    What flesh and blood can ne'er reveal,
Thy co-eternal Son display,
And call my darkness into day.

The gift unspeakable impart,
    Command the light of faith to shine,
To shine in my dark drooping heart,
    And fill me with the life divine;
Now bid the new creation be,
O God, let there be faith in me!

Thee without faith I cannot please:
    Faith without thee I cannot have:
But thou hast sent the Prince of Peace
    To seek my wandering soul, and save:
O Father! Glorify thy Son,
And save me for his sake alone!

Save me through faith in Jesus' blood,
    That blood which he for all did shed:
For me, for me, thou know'st, it flowed,
    For me, for me thou hear'st it plead;
Assure me now my soul is thine,
And all thou art in Christ is mine!
                    (*Redemption Hymns*, Hymn 14)

Reflect

We have seen how God illuminates the soul with the gift of
faith. God restores sight to the blind and rescues those who dwell

in darkness. Those who entrust their lives to God through Christ by faith pray for all the fullness of God in their lives. One of Charles Wesley's "redemption hymns" celebrates this portrait of life in Christ and draws us ever upward to the amazing gift of faith working through love. In this hymn we see precisely how faith works in our lives and how God brings about new creation through this gracious gift.

Wesley begins the drama of redemption with God and not with us. Jesus, our friend and advocate, loved and "died for me." Despite the fact that Christ has won our trust, entrusting our lives to him is hard, even when the Spirit makes him known. The second stanza articulates a central Wesleyan concept. Grace initiates the process of redemption, God reaching out to us with "alluring grace" even before we are capable of response. Our whole existence is enveloped in God's grace. Grace convicts us of our lack of faith, reveals the "smiling face" of Jesus, and calls us out of the darkness into God's marvelous light. Stanza three plays with this image of light. Wesley paints masterful word pictures and draws out the connection between redemption and creation in the biblical narrative. In creation, God sings, "Let there be light." In redemption, God commands "the light of faith to shine." The concluding couplet emphasizes the inseparable nature of God's grace in creation and redemption: "Now bid the new creation be, O God, let there be faith in me!"

Wesley begins stanza four with an amazing turn of phrase: "Thee without faith I cannot please: Faith without thee I cannot have." The gift of faith restores our fellowship with God. If we fail to put our trust in God, we remain alienated, unhappy, and insecure in life—a state of being hardly pleasing to the Creator who loves us. But the wonder of God's plan of redemption is that God supplies all we need but cannot provide for ourselves. Without God, faith could never be awakened in our soul. In the concluding lines of this stanza, Wesley describes the "prevenient" nature of God's grace once again. Prevenient simply means "that which comes before." Before anything else, God reaches out to us with grace and love. God sends "the Prince to Peace to seek my wandering soul, and save."

The final stanza celebrates two theological convictions of the Wesleys: 1) God's grace flows to all people; God excludes no one from this offer of relationship; 2) God's grace is "for me." *Because* Jesus died for *all*, he died for *me*! The repetition of that exclamation "For me, for me" underscores the profound personal dimension of life in Christ.

But Wesley mitigates against any exclusively subjective, individualistic, or sentimental view of redemption. The Authorized (or King James) Version of Wesley's day rendered 2 Corinthians 5:17: "Therefore if any man be in Christ, he is a *new creature.*" Anticipating more recent translations, Wesley's lyrical paraphrase suggests "If anyone is in Christ— new creation!" Through cross and resurrection, God births a whole new cosmic order that revolves around this pre-eminent act of love.

Pray

God of creation and re-creation, you offer us life in Jesus Christ through the gift of faith: Through the power of your Holy Spirit, enable us to embrace your gift and participate in the new creation you have brought into being throughout this universe. Amen.

SATURDAY IN LENT III

Read

So then, brothers and sisters, we are debtors, not to the flesh, to live according to the flesh—for if you live according to the flesh, you will die; but if by the Spirit you put to death the deeds of the body, you will live. For all who are led by the Spirit of God are children of God. For you did not receive a spirit of slavery to fall back into fear, but you have received a spirit of adoption. When we cry, "Abba! Father!" it is that very Spirit bearing witness with our spirit that we are children of God, and if children, then heirs, heirs of God and joint heirs with Christ—if, in fact, we suffer with him so that we may also be glorified with him. (Romans 8:12–17)

Sing

Meter: 886.886

This hymn can be sung to "Cornwall," the tune used for "We Sing of God, the Mighty Source."

> Thou great mysterious God unknown,
> Whose love hath gently led me on
>   E'en from my infant days,

Mine inmost soul expose to view,
And tell me if I never knew
    Thy justifying grace.

If I have only known thy fear,
And followed with a heart sincere
    Thy drawings from above,
Now, now the farther grace bestow,
And let my sprinkled conscience know
    Thy sweet forgiving love.

Short of thy love I would not stop,
A stranger to the gospel hope,
    The sense of sin forgiven,
I would not, Lord, my soul deceive,
Without thy inward witness live,
    That antepast of heaven.

If now the witness were in me,
Would he not testify of thee
    In Jesus reconciled?
And should I not with faith draw nigh,
And boldly Abba Father cry,
    I know myself thy child.

Ah never let thy servant rest,
Till of my part in Christ possessed
    I on thy mercy feed,
Unworthy of the crumbs that fall,
Yet raised by him who died for all
    To eat the children's bread.

O may I cast my rags aside,
My filthy rags of virtuous pride,
    And for acceptance groan;
My works and righteousness disclaim,
With all I have, or can, or am,
    And trust in grace alone.

Whate'er obstructs thy pardoning love,
Or sin, or righteousness remove,
   Thy glory to display,
Mine heart of unbelief convince,
And now absolve me from my sins,
   And take them all away.

Father, in me reveal thy Son,
And to my inmost soul make known
   How merciful thou art,
The secret of thy love reveal,
And by thine hallowing Spirit dwell
   Forever in my heart.
          (*Redemption Hymns*, Hymn 19)

Reflect

British Methodists have sometimes summarized the Wesleyan theology of salvation in a simple, four-fold statement: All people need to be saved. All people can be saved. All people can know they are saved. All people can be saved to the uttermost. These statements point respectively to the universality of sin, the unlimited offer of redemption, the assurance of salvation, and the full restoration of love in the life of the believer. As we come to the close of this week, having focused on the theme of groaning for full redemption, we look at the third element of this Wesleyan scheme, the conception of Christian assurance.

Both John and Charles Wesley loved this Romans 8 text. John included two sermons on the "witness of the Spirit" based upon this passage in his so-called "standard" collection. Charles's hymn might be described appropriately as a lyrical exposition of this text and theme. The first two stanzas of the hymn focus on the question, "How do we know that we belong to Christ?" None of us, of course, has ever seen God. God remains, on many levels, the "great mysterious God unknown," to use Wesley's own words. The fact that Charles had felt the love of God gently leading him as far back as he could remember saved him from a faithless and hopeless agnosticism. While he had never seen God, he had felt God's love.

He also realized that there are different kinds of knowing. Around the same time that Charles wrote this hymn, his older brother made an important distinction concerning the way we relate to God that may be reflected in the second stanza of the hymn. Reminiscing on the years prior to his experience of the witness of the Spirit in his life, John acknowledges that he felt and acted like a "servant of God," whereas after the Spirit enabled him to cry, "Abba, Father," he knew himself to be a "child of God." Servants know through fear; children know through love. And so Wesley prays in the hymn for a "farther grace"—the urgent need for which he signals by the repeated "now"—so that he might know "God's sweet forgiving love." While both servants and children dwell together in the same household, the relationship they experience with the parent is markedly different, and Wesley yearned for all to discover their true identity as the children of God.

Stanza five contains powerful images related to the family meal. Wesley's allusion to the liturgy of the *Book of Common Prayer* ("unworthy of the crumbs that fall") make it clear that Eucharistic imagery related to the Christian family meal was not far from his mind. Meals provide opportunity for our most intimate connections in life—places where we really know one another and come to know God. It is here that God offers "the children's bread" to all. Not wanting to leave any unsatisfied by simply knowing "about God," Wesley's prayer is that all might "know God" even as they are known. "Make known in my inmost soul, O God," the singer prays, "how merciful you are. Reveal your secret love, and dwell in my heart through the power of your Spirit forever."

Pray

Make known in our inmost soul, Abba, Father, how merciful you are; bear witness with our spirit that we are children of God, and if children, then heirs, heirs of God and joint heirs with Christ, through the power of your Spirit. Amen.

LENT IV: GOD'S GIFT OF LIBERATION

THE FOURTH SUNDAY IN LENT

Read

Then Moses and the Israelites sang this song to the Lord: "I will sing to the Lord, for he has triumphed gloriously; horse and rider he has thrown into the sea. The Lord is my strength and my might, and he has become my salvation; this is my God, and I will praise him, my father's God, and I will exalt him. The Lord is a warrior; the Lord is his name. Pharaoh's chariots and his army he cast into the sea; his picked officers were sunk in the Red Sea. The floods covered them; they went down into the depths like a stone. . . . You blew with your wind, the sea covered them; they sank like lead in the mighty waters. Who is like you, O Lord, among the gods? Who is like you, majestic in holiness, awesome in splendor, doing wonders? You stretched out your right hand, the earth swallowed them. In your steadfast love you led the people whom you redeemed; you guided them by your strength to your holy abode. . . ." And Miriam sang to them: "Sing to the Lord, for he has triumphed gloriously; horse and rider he has thrown into the sea." (Exodus 15:1–5, 10–13, 21)

Sing

Meter: 888.888

This hymn can be sung to "Melita," the tune used for "Almighty Father, Strong to Save."

> Arm of the Lord, awake for me!
> Art thou not it that smote the sea,
>> And all its mighty waters dried!
> Art thou not it that quelled the boast
> Of haughty Pharaoh, and his host,
>> And baffled all their furious pride!

78

Thou didst th'outrageous dragon wound,
Thou hast the horse and rider drowned,
   Glorious and excellent in power;
While Israel marched in firm array,
Triumphant through the wondrous way,
   Nor stumbled till they reached the shore.

Awake, as in the ancient days:
See in our foes th'Egyptian race,
   With hell's grim tyrant at their head,
Enraged at our escape he roars,
And follows us with all his powers,
   Out of his iron furnace freed.

"I will pursue, I will o'ertake,
I will my fugitives bring back,
   And satisfy my lust of blood,
Draw out my sword of keenest lies,
Pour a whole flood of perjuries,
   And make the rebels know their god."

Angel divine, who still art near,
Remove, and guard thy people's rear,
   This day for thy own Israel fight;
O let the pillar interpose,
A cloud and darkness to our foes,
   To us a flame of cheering light.

Hear us to thee for succor cry,
Nor let the hostile powers come nigh,
   In all our night of doubts and fears:
They cannot force their way through thee,
And thou shalt our protection be,
   Till the glad morning light appears.

Look through the tutelary cloud,
In which thou dost our souls enshroud,

And blast the aliens with thine eye,
Trouble the proud Egyptian host,
Confound their vain presumptuous boast
    Who Israel's God in us defy.

Arrest our fierce pursuers' speed,
Take off their chariot wheels, with dread
    And heavy wrath their spirits pain,
Extort the cry from ev'ry heart,
"Jehovah takes his people's part,
    We fight against the Lord in vain."
                    (*Redemption Hymns*, Hymn 12)

Reflect

The God of the scriptures is the God who acts. For the ancient Jews, salvation meant deliverance, liberation from all those forces that opposed Jahweh. Above all else, the Hebrew people confessed that the God-who-is-one liberates. Early in the book of Exodus, Jahweh declares: "I have come down to deliver them from the Egyptians and to bring them up out of that land to a good and broad land, a land flowing with milk and honey" (3:8). Memories of God's acts of liberation and the ongoing experience of deliverance in life by God's hand led the Psalmist to break into song. "You are a hiding place for me; you preserve me from trouble; you surround me with glad cries of deliverance" (32:7). In Psalm 68, he sings: "Our God is a God of salvation, and to God, the Lord, belongs escape from death" (20). The word for "salvation" in this song of liberation is the very same word for "deliverance." Psalm 18 (described as "A Psalm of David . . . when the Lord delivered him from the hand of all his enemies") celebrates the Savior who delivers: "The Lord is my rock, my fortress, and my deliverer, my God, my rock in whom I take refuge" (2). In the long history of Israel, the two most crucial defining events were the exodus from Egypt and the giving of the Law at Mt. Sinai. The Book of Exodus describes and interprets God's action to liberate a band of slaves from bondage and to shape them into a covenant community with Jahweh, the great Deliverer. Savior equals deliverer. Salvation equals liberation.

At the annual celebration of the Passover meal in the Jewish home, the spiritual heirs of this great legacy remember the Exodus.

This memory, however, is not a simple remembrance of events that lie long past in the history of the people; rather, the liberation experienced by their ancestors becomes their reality now. This "anamnetic" (from the Greek *anamnesis*, "remembrance") vision brings the past to life in the present moment. Their deliverance becomes our deliverance. As God acted in the past, so God acts now to liberate and to save. Charles Wesley exercised this specific form of remembrance in his hymn, which actually does little more than recall the details of the story of the Exodus itself. But it only takes a few words to bring this narrative—and its power to liberate—to life for us today. The opening line signals the "anamnesis" that Wesley intended. "Arm of the Lord, awake *for me!*" The hymn functions as a prayer for deliverance in the present based upon the affirmation of how God has acted in the past. Wesley repeats his supplication for God to "awake" in the third stanza. "Awake, as in the ancient days." "*Our* foes" displace the Egyptians; the Enemy replaces Pharaoh; ancient Israel becomes the faithful of God under attack right now. "*This day,*" Wesley pleads, "for thy own Israel fight." Jehovah heard the cry of the Chosen and delivered them; God liberates us now!

Pray

Great Deliverer, you liberated your people from bondage in Egypt and led them to a land flowing with milk and honey: Free us this day from all those forces that hold us in bondage and create barriers to the fullness of life we have in you. Amen.

MONDAY IN LENT IV

Read

I love you, O Lord, my strength. The Lord is my rock, my fortress, and my deliverer, my God, my rock in whom I take refuge, my shield, and the horn of my salvation, my stronghold. I call upon the Lord, who is worthy to be praised; so I shall be saved from my enemies. . . . He reached down from on high, he took me; he drew me out of mighty waters. He delivered me from my strong enemy, and from those who hated me; for they were too mighty for me. They confronted me in the day of my calamity; but the Lord was my support. He brought me out into a broad place; he delivered me, because he delighted in me. . . . The Lord lives! Blessed be my rock, and exalted be the God of my salvation, the God who gave me vengeance and subdued peoples under me; who delivered me from my enemies; indeed, you exalted me above my adversaries; you delivered me from the violent. For this I will extol you, O Lord, among the nations, and sing praises to your name. (Psalm 18:1–3, 16–19, 46–49)

Sing

Meter: 87.87D

This hymn can be sung to "St. Columba," the tune used for "The King of Love My Shepherd Is."

> We bless our Lord with gratitude
> And strength ascribe to Jesus!
> Jesus alone
> Defends his own,
> When earth and hell oppress us.
> Jesus with joy we witness now
> Almighty to deliver,
> Our seal set to
> That God is true,
> And reigns a King for ever.

> Your arm has safely brought us through
> A way no more expected,
> Than when your sheep
> Passed through the deep,
> By crystal walls protected.
> Your glory was our strength and shield,
> Your hand our lives did cover,
> And we, e'en we
> Have walked the sea,
> And marched triumphant over.

> The world and Satan's malice sore
> You, Jesus, have confounded,

And by your grace
With songs of praise
Our happy souls resounded.
Accepting our deliverance
We triumph in your favor,
And for the love
Which now we prove,
Shall praise your name for ever.
(*Redemption Hymns*, Hymn 20.1, 3, 6)

Reflect

"Deliverer" was Charles Wesley's favorite name for the Savior. Our texts today continue the theme of deliverance. The biblical song of liberation appears not only here in the Psalter, but also in the account of David's final days in 2 Samuel 22. In its setting here as a Psalm, this song emphasizes the king's absolute dependence upon God. The second verse describes Yahweh with a string of predicates longer than any other in the Psalter. David describes the Lord as my rock, my fortress, my shield, my horn of my salvation, and my stronghold. Repeating the possessive pronoun "my" underscores both the radical nature of his dependence upon God and the intimate nature of their relationship. In the setting of this song in 2 Samuel, the community generalizes the thanksgiving for this particular experience of victory, interpreting the one event theologically and expanding it to embrace all experiences of salvation, both present and in the future. This twist emphasizes the fact that God has not only *saved* in the past, but God *saves* and *will save*.

I experienced this confession of faith in a dramatic way in the summer of 1986. I was attending the World Methodist Conference in Nairobi, Kenya. Bishop Desmond Tutu addressed the assembly one afternoon in a packed session. This was at the height of his struggle against the racist and unjust apartheid regime in South Africa. He spoke of his experience in the midst of that battle against evil. He claimed his vision of a free South Africa because, as he confessed, the God he had come to know in Jesus Christ was a God of justice. At the climactic moment of the address he waved his Bible in his hand over his head and exclaimed, "Apartheid is dead. Apartheid is dead." Long before it toppled, God had already defeated it. Later that evening, a special banquet was held in his honor and I had the great privilege of being only several yards away from him. As the guests began to arrive, a choir from South Africa broke its way through the crowd and serenaded Bishop Tutu with the songs of liberation that he knew so well. He sang with them and danced because he knew that God would triumph in the end, and God did.

In the history of biblical interpretation since the time of the early church, Christians have understood the king of Psalm 18 as a type of Christ. This song, and all others like it that identify salvation with deliverance, give potent expression to a classic concept of atonement oriented around the victory of Christ over the powers of death, sin, and evil in this world. These forces separate us from God, but the redemptive work of Christ frees us from their grasp, gives us the victory, and sets us free to serve the God of justice, righteousness, and love. Jesus has confounded "the world and Satan's malice." So let us dance and sing the song of deliverance, for Christ has freed us for joyful obedience.

Pray

Liberating God, you have delivered us from death, sin, and evil through the redemptive work of Christ: Help us to embrace the freedom that you so graciously offer to us this day. Amen.

TUESDAY IN LENT IV

Read

I will bless the Lord at all times; his praise shall continually be in my mouth. My soul makes its boast in the Lord; let the humble hear and be glad. O magnify the Lord with me, and let us exalt his name together. I sought the Lord, and he answered me, and delivered me from all my fears. Look to him, and be radiant; so your faces shall never be ashamed. This poor soul cried, and was heard by the Lord, and was saved from every trouble. The angel of the Lord encamps around those who fear him, and delivers them. O taste and see that the Lord is good; happy are those who take refuge in him. (Psalm 34:1–8)

Sing
Unusual Meter: 555.11.555.11
No contemporary tune.

> All thanks be to God,
> Who scatters abroad
> Throughout every place,
> By the least of his servants his savor of grace!
> Who the victory gave,
> The praise let him have,
> For the work he hath done,
> All honor and glory to Jesus alone.

> Our conquering Lord
> Hath prospered the word,
> Hath made it prevail,
> And mightily shaken the kingdom of hell:
> His arm he hath bared,
> And a people prepared,
> His glory to show,
> And witness the power of his Passion below.

> He hath opened a door
> To the penitent poor,
> And rescued from sin,
> And admitted the harlots and publicans in:
> They have heard the glad sound,
> They have liberty found
> Through the blood of the Lamb,
> And plentiful pardon in Jesus's name.

> And shall we not sing
> Our Savior and King?
> Thy witnesses, we
> With rapture ascribe our salvation to thee.
> Thou Jesus hast blessed,
> And believers increased,

Who thankfully own
We are freely forgiven through mercy alone.

Thy Spirit revives
His work in our lives,
His wonders of grace
So mightily wrought in the primitive days.
O that all men might know
Thy tokens below,
Our Savior confess,
And embrace the glad tidings of pardon and peace!
(*Redemption Hymns*, Hymn 3.1–3, 5–6)

Reflect

A striking and unique similarity connects Psalm 34 and Wesley's hymn. Both sing praise to God in the form of thanksgiving for help, but this is not their most significant connection. More importantly, they both function to instruct those who sing and hear these words in the way they are to be formed by God. With regard to the Psalm, attention is often given to the resemblance of this song with Psalm 25. But whereas the latter appears to be more liturgical in form, this Psalm serves a didactic purpose. This song, like Wesley's hymn, bears witness to what God does for us and in us; both expressions of praise teach the community of faith why we give thanks and how to give thanks with our lives.

The opening stanza of Wesley's hymn proclaims thanks to God for the victory God has won through Christ. But word of this victory must be shared with every person and in every place by those who have tasted and seen the honor and glory of Jesus.

Stanzas two and three describe what *Christ* has done *for us* in his great work of redemption. The "conquering Lord" prospered the word, prevailed, and has shaken the kingdom of hell. As a consequence, a part of our responsibility is to demonstrate the glory of Christ and witness to the power of his redeeming work. Jesus' acts on our behalf open, rescue, and admit. He demonstrated special concern for the poor. These beloved ones of God, in particular, have heard, have been liberated, and experience pardon. That great work that God does for us in Christ is the foundation of our life with God. It consists of the forgiveness of our sins and the restoration of our relationship with God. We experience Christ's work on our behalf in this regard as pardon—a "plentiful pardon in Jesus's name."

Jesus is the subject of these two stanzas, but stanza four shifts to "us." Wesley replaces "he" with "we" because of the important claim that Christ makes upon us all in the act of redemption. Those who have been restored to God in Christ are witnesses to all that God has done for us. We are called to own and proclaim the deliverance that is ours in the Lord.

In the final stanza, Wesley focuses our attention on the goal of the Christian life, on the work of the Holy Spirit in our lives—the work and the wonders "so mightily wrought." Having instructed the singer about what God does for us in Christ, he now describes what the *Spirit* is doing *in us* in God's great work of restoration. While intimately related to the foundation of faith in Christ, regeneration, or new birth, refers to what God does in us through the power of the Holy Spirit. Justification changes our relationship to God; new birth signals a real change in our lives. God not only forgives our sin through Christ, through the indwelling Spirit, God inscribes a new law of love in our hearts. Because of Jesus we are pardoned; in the Spirit we are filled increasingly with God's peace and love.

Pray

Conquering Lord, we give you thanks because you work for us through Christ and in us by the power of your Holy Spirit to restore our relationship with you and to shape us into a more loving people; help us to experience your pardon and peace on a daily basis. Amen.

WEDNESDAY IN LENT IV

Read

The crowd joined in attacking them, and the magistrates had them stripped of their clothing and ordered them to be beaten with rods. After they had given them a severe flogging, they threw them into prison and ordered the jailer to keep them securely. Following these instructions, he put them in the innermost cell and fastened their feet in the stocks. About midnight Paul and Silas were praying and singing hymns to God, and the prisoners were listening to them. Suddenly there was an earthquake, so violent that the foundations of the prison were shaken; and immediately all the doors were opened and everyone's chains were unfastened. When the jailer woke up and saw the prison doors wide open, he drew his sword and was about to kill himself, since he supposed that the prisoners had escaped. But Paul shouted in a loud voice, "Do not harm yourself, for we are all here." The jailer called for lights, and rushing in, he fell down trembling before Paul and Silas. Then he brought them outside and said, "Sirs, what must I do to be saved?" They answered, "Believe on the Lord Jesus, and you will be saved, you and your household." (Acts 16:11–31)

Sing
Meter: 88.88.88
This hymn can be sung to "St. Petersburg," the tune used for "Before Thy Throne, O God."

> And can it be, that I should gain
>> An interest in the Savior's blood!
> Died he for me?—Who caused his pain!
>> For me?—Who him to death pursued.
> Amazing love! How can it be
> That thou, my God, shouldst die for me?

> 'Tis mystery all! Th'immortal dies!
>> Who can explore his strange design?
> In vain the first born seraph tries
>> To sound the depths of love divine.
> 'Tis mercy all! Let earth adore;
> Let angel minds inquire no more.

> He left his Father's throne above,
>> (So free, so infinite his grace!)
> Emptied himself of all but love,
>> And bled for Adam's helpless race:
> 'Tis mercy all, immense and free!
> For O my God! It found out me!

Long my imprisoned spirit lay,
    Fast bound in sin and nature's night:
Thine eye diffused a quickening ray;
    I woke; the dungeon flamed with light;
My chains fell off, my heart was free,
I rose, went forth, and followed thee.

Still the small inward voice I hear,
    That whispers all my sins forgiven;
Still the atoning blood is near,
    That quenched the wrath of hostile heaven:
I feel the life his wounds impart;
I feel my Savior in my heart.

No condemnation now I dread,
    Jesus, and all in him, is mine:
Alive in him, my living head,
    And clothed in righteousness divine,
Bold I approach th'eternal throne,
And claim the crown, through Christ, my own.
                (*HSP* [(1739], pp. 117–19)

Reflect

Wesley's hymn originally entitled "Free Grace" is one of the most significant lyrical expositions of salvation in the history of Christian song. It may have been the so-called "conversion hymn" that he wrote immediately following his evangelical conversion of May 21, 1738. It also may have been the hymn that the brothers sang, according to John's journal, when he came late in the evening of May 24 to announce his own conversion to his younger brother. "And can it be" is a magisterial treatment of both the experience and theology of God's unconditional love and its effects on our lives.

The opening question is decisive for the whole of Wesley's theology. "And can it be, that I should gain an interest in the Savior's blood?" Today we would use the term "share" or "part" in place of Wesley's "interest." Could it possibly be that I could have some part in this amazing and costly drama of salvation? The questions that follow amplify the extraordinary nature and the full extent of God's love for us. How could Christ have died for the one who has caused him so much pain? I have crucified him just as surely as those who stood at the foot of the cross. "How can it be that thou, *my God*, shouldst die for me?" Wesley was overwhelmed! This is amazing love, indeed!

In the successive stanzas, he spells out in greater detail what the "share in his blood"—the cost of redemption means. Each insight is as overwhelming as the realization that floods over us in the opening stanza. The hymn is so tightly packed, hardly a part of it can be left out. The insight revealed in stanza two relates to the mystery of godliness. God loves us so much that in Jesus Christ, God dies—the immortal dies! No one is capable of understanding the depth of this mystery. Not even heavenly beings are able to "sound the depths" of this kind of love. All is mercy! All is gift! All we can do is stand in awe of this *agape* love that is willing to sacrifice all that we might live and love.

In stanza three Wesley condenses the whole doctrine of God's self-emptying in the act of Incarnation into a single line. He believes that *kenosis* (the technical term from Philippians. 2:7, meaning "to empty the self") is the key, in fact, to the mystery of God's love. In his *Hymns on the Lord's Supper* we sing, "He came self-emptied from above, that we might live through him" (Hymn 60). No image of kenosis impresses itself on our minds with greater force than Wesley's distinctive phrase, "Emptied himself of all but love." The wonder of it all, claims the poet, is that this One, emptied of all but love, "found out me!"

The next stanza is one of my personal favorites because it celebrates the liberation that Christ offers to us all. The allusions to the story of Paul and Silas in Acts 16 are unmistakable. How could any prose reflection improve this masterful and moving poetry:

> Long my imprisoned spirit lay,
>> Fast bound in sin and nature's night:
> Thine eye diffused a quickening ray;
>> I woke; the dungeon flamed with light;
> My chains fell off, my heart was free,
> I rose, went forth, and followed thee.

"The sheer sense of wonder that it should happen 'to me,'" as my mentor in Wesley studies often said, "never left the master poet." May it be so for us!

Pray

Self-emptying God, we are overwhelmed by the extent of your love. Open our hearts and lives to the power of your love that our chains fall off and our hearts are set free. Amen.

Thursday in Lent IV

Read

Now the Lord is the Spirit, and where the Spirit of the Lord is, there is freedom. And all of us, with unveiled faces, seeing the glory of the Lord as though reflected in a mirror, are being transformed into the same image from one degree of glory to another; for this comes from the Lord, the Spirit. (2 Corinthians 3:17–18)

Sing

Meter: SM

The hymn can be sung to "St. Michael," the tune used for "O Day of God, Draw Nigh."

> Come then, and dwell in me,
> Spirit of power within,
> And bring the glorious liberty
> From sorrow, fear, and sin:
> The seed of sin's disease,
> Spirit of health, remove,
> Spirit of finished holiness,
> Spirit of perfect love.
>
> Hasten the joyful day
> Which shall my sins consume,
> When old things shall be past away,
> And all things new become;
> The original offence
> Out of my heart erase,
> Enter O God and drive it hence,
> And take up all the place.

I want the witness, Lord,
That all I do is right,
According to your mind and word,
Well pleasing in your sight:
I seek no higher state,
Indulge me but in this,
And soon, or later then translate
To your eternal bliss.

(*Scripture Hymns*, vol. 2,
Hymns 298, 301, 367)

Reflect

When I was in high school our choir sang one of the classic choral works of the Norwegian composer and pianist Edvard Grieg. The climax of this masterpiece comes with the repetition of those powerful words, "God's Son has made me free. God's Son has made me free. Yes free; yes, free; free, free, free. God's Son has made me free." At the time, I was experiencing important breakthroughs in my own spiritual life and I felt that freedom in the depths of my soul. I wanted everyone who sang those words to experience the same liberation and joy. I could hardly sing without getting choked up.

In that portion of St. Paul's Second Letter to the Corinthians from which our text for today is taken, the Apostle discusses God's glory and the way in which that glory is reflected in the lives of the faithful. He contrasts the old glory to the new glory that has broken into history in the person of Jesus. He develops this characteristic theme of the old and the new, a theme that comes to a climax in chapter five where he discusses the new creation. Paul identifies this new and "greater glory" with the Spirit, who is the Risen Christ. The primary characteristic of this Spirit/Christ-expressed glory is freedom. "Now the Lord is the Spirit, and where the Spirit of the Lord is, there is freedom." How liberating this message must have been, especially as the young Christians of the Corinthian community pondered Paul's vision that they were being "transformed into the same image from one degree of glory to another." In his great hymn "Love Divine, All Loves Excelling," Wesley drew upon these same images as he described life in Christ as a process of being "changed from glory into glory."

Wesley celebrates the glory of freedom in the Spirit. The Spirit that indwells our lives is a spirit of power, health, holiness, and perfect love.

The glorious liberty that accompanies the Spirit frees us from sorrow, fear, and sin. In the practice of the "Jesus prayer" from the Eastern Orthodox tradition, the words, "Lord Jesus Christ, Son of God" accompany our breathing in, while we say, "have mercy on me, a sinner" as we slowly release our breath. Practice this prayer right now. Relax, and while you inhale, say "Lord Jesus Christ" (embracing the health, holiness, and love that the Spirit offers). As you exhale continue with "have mercy on me," and let go of sorrow, fear, and sin. Relinquish them to the Spirit, and with your next breath embrace the power of the Spirit to set you free.

In the closing stanzas of the hymn we encounter what the spiritual writers describe as an apophatic (emptying) and kataphatic (filling) rhythm. As in the breathing prayer, we permit the Spirit to empty us of the old and fill us with the new. The Spirit consumes, blots out, erases, and drives out our sins, emptying us of all that separates us from God; the Spirit fills us with the mind and righteousness of Christ, witnessing with our spirits that we are the children of God. Throughout the course of the day, experience the freedom that God offers you through the Spirit, emptying yourself and then being filled with love, over and over again.

Pray

Spirit of Freedom, blot out my transgressions and drive out all my latent desires to sin so that I might be filled with the power of your presence and the freedom to truly live and love again. Amen.

FRIDAY IN LENT IV

Read

Then I saw a new heaven and a new earth; for the first heaven and the first earth had passed away, and the sea was no more. And I saw the holy city, the new Jerusalem, coming down out of heaven from God, prepared as a bride adorned for her husband. And I heard a loud voice from the throne saying, "See, the home of God is among mortals. He will dwell with them; they will be his peoples, and God himself will be with them; he will wipe every tear from their eyes. Death will be no more; mourning and crying and pain will be no more, for the first things have passed away." (Revelation 21:1–4)

Sing

Meter: 66.66.88

This hymn can be sung to "Darwall's 148th," the tune used for "Ye Holy Angels Bright."

> Jesus, accept the praise
> That to your name belongs,
> Matter of all our lays,
> Subject of all our songs,
> Through you we now together came,
> And part exulting in your name.
>
> In flesh we part a while
> (But still in spirit joined)
> To embrace the happy toil
> You have for each assigned:
> And while we do your blessed will,
> We bear our heaven about us still.
>
> O let us thus go on,
> In all your pleasant ways,
> And, armed with patience, run
> With joy the appointed race:
> Keep us, and every seeking soul,
> Till all attain the heavenly goal.
>
> There we shall meet again,
> When all our toils are o'er,
> And death, and grief, and pain,
> And parting is no more:
> We shall with all your children rise,
> And grasp you in the flaming skies.
>
> O happy, happy day,
> That calls your exiles home!
> The heavens shall pass away,
> The earth receive its doom,
> Earth we shall view, and heaven destroyed,
> And shout above the fiery void.

These eyes shall see them fall,
    Mountains, and stars, and skies,
These eyes shall see them all
    Out of their ashes rise;
These lips his praises shall rehearse,
Whose nod restores the universe.

According to his word,
    His oath to sinners given,
We look to see restored
    The ruined earth and heaven,
In a new world his truth to prove,
A world of righteousness and love.

Then let us wait the sound
    That shall our souls release,
And labor to be found
    Of him in spotless peace,
In perfect holiness renewed,
Adorned with Christ, and meet for God.
                  (*Redemption Hymns*, Hymn 48)

Reflect

Death is our final enemy. But Jesus has already delivered us from death! As St. Paul wrote to the Corinthians, "Death has been swallowed up in victory. Where, O death, is your victory? Where, O death, is your sting?" (1 Cor. 15:54–5) Surrounding the deathbed of their mother, John Wesley and his sisters may have sung one of Charles's funeral hymns which included the triumphant confession: "Fought the fight, the work is done, death is swallowed up [in] life." One simple couplet from Wesley's hymn for today identifies four enemies from which Jesus delivers us: "And death, and grief, and pain, and parting is no more." This echoes the amazing vision of John's Revelation in which God "will wipe every tear from their eyes. Death will be no more; mourning and crying and pain will be no more" (21:4).

Death. Three deaths have hit me very hard in my life. Just as I was preparing to leave seminary for my first position in pastoral ministry, my wife and I lost our son, Jonathan, to stillbirth. He would have been my only son. Death stole him from us, and all our hopes and dreams that surrounded his birth crumbled. It was one of the darkest periods in our lives. Later, my dear parents died within about a year of each other. They were unbelievably godly people who had dedicated their lives to Christ and his ministry. As you have heard my story, I am sure that the faces of your own loved ones have flashed before your eyes. Death surrounded Jesus; a little girl, a widow's only son, a dear friend.

Grief. Every loss in life brings its own grief. All losses, great or small, remind us of our own mortality. Lent confronts us unapologetically with this reality from which we shrink. We all grieve. Some experiences in life wound us deeply. We deny them. We bargain our way through them with God, seeking some resolution of the pain we feel. Grief sometimes sweeps over us at the least expected moment and we simply can do nothing but cry. Jesus wept.

Pain. All of these losses hurt deeply. Pain is not simply a physical reality. One of our friends who is a neurologist and expert about pain has told us that pain continues to baffle scientists in many ways. At best, we manage it. One thing is certain, we all prefer pleasure to pain. But, like it or not, agony accompanies us on our journey through life. Jesus suffered under Pontius Pilate.

Parting. It is hard to say goodbye, especially to those we love. One of my colleagues is a Navy Reserve chaplain. He was deployed recently for service in Iraq. He will be gone for more than a year. I can only imagine the pain and anxiety associated with his departure. Life involves a cycle of beginnings and endings, greeting and leave-taking. Jesus had to part with those he loved.

Wesley's hymn reminds us that God in Christ has triumphed over death, grief, pain, and parting. Our confidence and hope in this most critical of victories does not diminish the grief of the present moment, perhaps, or fully ease the pain related to the finitude of life, but it does encourage us to move forward with hope and to run with patience the race before us. In Jesus, all these enemies are all swallowed up in life with God.

Pray

Eternal God, because of Christ's victory, we can cry out, "Where, O death, is your victory? Where, O death is your sting?" Sustain us in our journey until we are all in all in you. Amen.

SATURDAY IN LENT IV

Read

I pray that, according to the riches of his glory, he may grant that you may be strengthened in your inner being with power through his Spirit, and that Christ may dwell in your hearts through faith, as you are being rooted and grounded in love. I pray that you may have the power to comprehend, with all the saints, what is the breadth and length and height and depth, and to know the love of Christ that surpasses knowledge, so that you may be filled with all the fullness of God. Now to him who by the power at work within us is able to accomplish abundantly far more than all we can ask or imagine, to him be glory in the church and in Christ Jesus to all generations, forever and ever. Amen. (Ephesians 3:16–21)

Sing

Meter: CM

This hymn can be sung to "Azmon," the tune used for "O For a Thousand Tongues to Sing."

> Jesus, thine all-victorious love
> Shed in my heart abroad;
> Then shall my feet no longer rove
> Rooted and fixed in God.
>
> Love only can the conquest win,
> The strength of sin subdue,
> (Mine own unconquerable sin)
> And form my soul anew.
>
> Love can bow down the stubborn neck,
> The stone to flesh convert,
> Soften, and melt, and pierce, and break
> An adamantine heart.
>
> O that in me the sacred fire
> Might now begin to glow,

Burn up the dross of base desire,
    And make the mountains flow!

O that it now from heaven might fall,
    And all my sins consume!
Come, Holy Ghost, for thee I call,
    Spirit of burning come!

Refining fire, go through my heart,
    Illuminate my soul,
Scatter thy life through every part,
    And sanctify the whole.

No longer then my heart shall mourn,
    While purified by grace,
I only for his glory burn,
    And always see his face.

My steadfast soul, from falling free,
    Can now no longer move;
Jesus is all the world to me,
    And all my heart is love.
        (*HSP* [1740], pp. 157–58, vv. 4–9, 11–12)

Reflect

No force in the universe is more powerful than love. If we ask the question "What is it that makes Jesus' deliverance possible?" the answer is clear. As Wesley confessed: "Love only can the conquest win." Love is more powerful than hate. Love triumphs over evil. Love can conquer the disobedient heart. Love never coerces. Love never fails. St. Paul explores the dimensions of the amazing love in his letter to the Ephesians. In a book entitled *Recapturing the Wesleys' Vision*, I use this text as a framework for the theology of the Wesleys.

For them, everything began with the *height* of sovereign grace—with the message of God's good news in Jesus Christ revealed in the story of his death and resurrection. Our encounter with this gospel immediately draws us into a community where we can learn how to love by experiencing the *depth* of genuine and caring relationships.

In the context of this new family and throughout the *length* of the Christian journey, those who learn of Christ receive the discipline that is necessary for them to be nourished and grow in their faith. All Christians, however, find their ultimate purpose in servanthood, in the *breadth* of compassionate witness.

Just as in Jesus' image of the vine and the branches in John 15, we are gathered together to learn how to love (disciples) and then sent out into the world (apostles) to share that love with others. If love is the key to the way of Jesus, then it must also unlock the door to our faithfulness. To use a familiar image, think for a moment about a wheel and the forces that make it spin. The *centripetal* force, which persistently draws all things toward the center or hub, is joined with an opposing *centrifugal* force that thrusts out toward the rim. The wheel of the Christian life turns as we are both centered in Jesus and sent in his name into the world in mission. We need both forces in our lives if we are going to live by Christ's law of love. This is how God cultivates a reciprocal love in our lives so that the love of Christ might work through us in God's world.

Charles Wesley prayed consistently for God's love to fill his soul, and not his soul only, but the soul of every child of God. His hymn celebrates the experience of divine love and the working of the Holy Spirit—the way in which we both know and feel God in our lives. The Spirit fills our hearts with God's all-victorious love. This love is like a fire that converts, softens, melts, pierces, breaks, glows, burns, consumes, refines, illuminates, fills, and sanctifies our souls. God's all-victorious love firmly roots and fixes us in Christ. Wesley's prayer is that all might experience this in life. Make his prayer your own this day. Pray that you might know and feel God's all-victorious love.

Pray

Refining Fire, go through my heart, illuminate my soul, scatter thy life through every part, and sanctify the whole: Grant that Jesus may be all the world to me, and then, all my heart will be filled with God's all-victorious love. Amen.

Lent V: Rejoicing in Grace

The Fifth Sunday in Lent

Read

You will say in that day: I will give thanks to you, O Lord, for though you were angry with me, your anger turned away, and you comforted me. Surely God is my salvation; I will trust, and will not be afraid, for the Lord God is my strength and my might; he has become my salvation. With joy you will draw water from the wells of salvation. And you will say in that day: "Give thanks to the Lord, call on his name; make known his deeds among the nations; proclaim that his name is exalted. Sing praises to the Lord, for he has done gloriously; let this be known in all the earth. Shout aloud and sing for joy, O royal Zion, for great in your midst is the Holy One of Israel." (Isaiah 12)

Sing

Meter: 77.77

This hymn can be sung to "Savannah," the tune used for "Love's Redeeming Work is Done."

> Happy soul who sees the day,
>   The glad day of gospel grace!
> Thee my Lord (thou then wilt say)
>   Thee will I forever praise.
>
> Me behold! Thy mercy spares,
>   Jesus my salvation is:
> Hence my doubts, away my fears,
>   Jesus is become my peace.
>
> Mine; and yours, whoe'er believe:
>   On his name whoe'er shall call,

Freely shall his grace receive;
     He is full of grace for all.

Therefore shall you draw with joy
     Water from salvation's well,
Praise shall your glad tongues employ,
     While God's streaming grace you feel.

Each to each, you then shall say,
     Sinners, call on Jesus' name,
O rejoice to see his day,
     See it, and his praise proclaim.

Glory to his name belongs,
     Great, and marvelous, and high,
Sing unto the Lord your songs,
     Cry, to every nation, cry.

Wondrous things the Lord hath done,
     Excellent God's name we find,
This to humankind is known:
     Known to all of humankind.

Zion, shout thy Lord and King,
     Israel's holy one is he,
Give him thanks, rejoice, and sing,
     Great he is, and dwells in thee.

O the grace unsearchable!
     While eternal ages roll,
Christ delights in us to dwell,
     Soul of each believing soul.
               (*HSP* [1742], pp. 189–90, vv. 1, 3, 6–12)

Reflect

John Calvin argued that gratitude is the primary characteristic of the Christian. The believer cannot help but sing praises to God, give thanks and sing of God's greatness, mercy, and love. When all is said and done, everything rests in God's grace. An early Methodist woman bore testimony to this fact on her deathbed. She said that she had heard many people talk about being faithful to the grace of God as if they trusted in their own faithfulness. She would hear none of this. She maintained that it was God's faithfulness to his own word of promise that was her only security for salvation. She believed in grace.

The prophet Isaiah cries out and shouts this glorious message. God's grace, he declares, is like a deep, deep well that never runs dry and from which we can draw the water of salvation. Knut Nystedt's masterful choral composition based upon this text, "Cry Out and Shout," bursts with excitement. It opens with voices simulating an Aaron Copeland–style brass fanfare. "Cry out and shout ye people of God." It makes you want to shout: "God is our strength; God is our song." Therefore! With joy we draw water from the wells of salvation. In the ancient world, "life-giving water" symbolized Jahweh's saving power. Moreover, at that time, just as in many parts of Africa today, daily trips to the well were the common tasks of life. Every dip of the bucket reminds the believer that the gracious God saves. A rough equivalent for us might be the turn of the water tap. Every time that water flows, is it not a reminder that God is good and gracious and anxious to save?

Stanza three of Wesley's hymn proclaims two important things about God's grace, both characteristic of the Wesleyan understanding of God. First, this grace is for all. God gladly enters into a life-giving relationship with whoever believes, with whoever calls upon God's name. Second, grace fills God. There is nothing about God, in other words, that is not gracious. God can be nothing but grace because love is God's essence.

In three other stanzas, Wesley adds adjectives to more fully express the significance of God's grace. We draw "Gospel grace" out of the wells. God's grace is good news. It springs out of the "Christ well." We draw "streaming grace" out of the wells. God's grace flows freely; it is always on the move, bubbling up, living. It springs out of the "Spirit well." We draw "grace unsearchable" out of the wells. We cannot fathom the depths of this well. God's love—God's grace—is too deep and too wondrous. It springs from the "Creator well."

There is a profound evangelistic implication in this exclamation of praise concerning the God of grace. Isaiah makes this very clear. If you have drawn water from these wells, then you must point others to this life-giving source. We are called to "make known his deeds among the nations" and to "let this be known in all the earth." Therefore . . . cry out and shout ye people of God, the Lord our strength and song! Draw water from the wells of salvation! Cry out and shout ye people of God!

Pray

I will give thanks to you, O Lord, for you are my strength and my song; with joy I will draw water from the wells of salvation, for you have done gloriously and your grace overflows for all. Amen.

Monday in Lent V

Read

The days are surely coming, says the Lord, when I will make a new covenant with the house of Israel and the house of Judah. It will not be like the covenant that I made with their ancestors when I took them by the hand to bring them out of the land of Egypt—a covenant that they broke, though I was their husband, says the Lord. But this is the covenant that I will make with the house of Israel after those days, says the Lord: I will put my law within them, and I will write it on their hearts; and I will be their God, and they shall be my people. (Jeremiah 31:31–33)

Sing

Meter: CM

This hymn can be sung to "Richmond," the tune used for "Hark! the Glad Sound."

> O for a heart to praise my God,
>   A heart from sin set free!
> A heart that always feels thy blood,
>   So freely spilt for me!
>
> A heart resigned, submissive, meek,
>   My dear Redeemer's throne,

Where only Christ is heard to speak,
 Where Jesus reigns alone.

An humble, lowly, contrite heart,
 Believing, true, and clean,
Which neither life nor death can part
 From him that dwells within.

A heart in every thought renewed,
 And full of love divine,
Perfect, and right, and pure and good,
 A copy, Lord, of thine.

Thy tender heart is still the same,
 And melts at human woe:
Jesu, for thee distressed I am,
 I want thy love to know.

My heart, thou knowest can never rest,
 Till thou create my peace,
Till of my Eden repossessed,
 From self, and sin I cease.

Fruit of thy gracious lips, on me
 Bestow that peace unknown,
The hidden manna, and the tree
 Of life, and the white stone.

Thy nature, dearest Lord, impart,
 Come quickly from above,
Write thy new name upon my heart,
 Thy new, best name of love.
    (*HSP* [1742], pp. 30–31)

Reflect

What is written on your heart? That may be a more significant question that you think. Whatever is written on our hearts reflects who we are on the deepest level. If "our hearts are not in it"—if we

are only "half-hearted" in our commitment—then we lack something essential. John Wesley preached a sermon entitled "The Almost
Christian." The thrust of his message was the importance of "whole-
hearted" trust in Christ and "whole-hearted" commitment to God's
reign. The prophet Jeremiah knew about the importance of the heart.
He loved the Law of God, but he looked forward to the day when
God's Law would be more than an external authority governing the
life of the people of God. He anticipated how God would act to transform the Law into a relational, personal, dynamic, internal force. God
will write the new covenant of love upon the hearts of God's people.

Wesley's hymn celebrates the heart of the believer—the heart
upon which God has written the Law of Love. Originally entitled
"Make me a clean Heart, O God" and based upon Psalm 51:10, this
poetic prayer represents one of his most powerful endorsements of
"heart religion." The foundation of this hymn, like the Psalm and like
Jeremiah's vision, is God's steadfast love and the covenant relationship
God offers to all whom God loves. Essentially, the hymn describes
the nature and qualities of the heart for which he prays. But note that
Wesley does not claim such a heart; rather, he realizes that "a copy"
of Christ's own heart can only be given. It is God who writes on the
heart, shapes the character, forms the disciple, restores the image of
Christ in the child. The consequence of God's action—the product
of God's activity—reflects the dimensions of God's grace applied to a
heart that is open to the spirit of Christ.

First and foremost, this heart is free. The heart in which Christ
reigns is resigned, submissive, and meek; humble, lowly, and contrite;
believing, true, and clean. None of these descriptions, however, implies
weakness; rather, our strength comes from understanding who we are
in proper relation to God. The humility of Christ functions as the primary foundation of every believer's life. Wesley piles the attributes on
top of one another in the hymn. God renews the heart and fills it with
love divine so that it reflects the perfect, right, pure, and good heart of
Christ. This tender heart empathizes with others, offers compassion,
and longs for peace. Wesley prays for God to "write thy new name
upon my heart, thy new, best name of love."

In the Sacrament of Holy Communion we especially remember the
new covenant and God's promise to us in Christ. The liturgy confirms
that God has made a "new covenant with us by water and the Spirit."

We participate in the "blood of the new covenant," poured out for all that our sins might be forgiven. We pray for the capacity to "perfectly love God" in the context of this new covenant relationship of love.

Pray

Covenant God, you are the one who reaches out to us to establish relationships of love: Come quickly from above, impart your nature and write your new name upon my heart, your new, best name of love. Amen.

TUESDAY IN LENT V

Read

Blessed be the God and Father of our Lord Jesus Christ! By his great mercy he has given us a new birth into a living hope through the resurrection of Jesus Christ from the dead, and into an inheritance that is imperishable, undefiled, and unfading, kept in heaven for you, who are being protected by the power of God through faith for a salvation ready to be revealed in the last time. In this you rejoice, even if now for a little while you have had to suffer various trials, so that the genuineness of your faith—being more precious than gold that, though perishable, is tested by fire—may be found to result in praise and glory and honor when Jesus Christ is revealed. Although you have not seen him, you love him; and even though you do not see him now, you believe in him and rejoice with an indescribable and glorious joy, for you are receiving the outcome of your faith, the salvation of your souls. (1 Peter 1:3–9)

Sing

Meter: 88.88.88

The hymn can be sung to "St. Petersburg," the tune used for "Before Thy Throne, O God."

> Thou hidden source of calm repose,
> Thou all-sufficient love divine,
> My help, and refuge from my foes,
> Secure I am, if thou art mine,

And lo! From sin, and grief, and shame
I hide me, Jesus, in thy name.

Thy mighty name salvation is,
        And keeps my happy soul above,
Comfort it brings, and power, and peace,
        And joy, and everlasting love:
To me with thy dear name are given
Pardon, and holiness, and heaven.

Jesu, my all in all thou art,
        My rest in toil, my ease in pain,
The med'cine of my broken heart,
        In war my peace, in loss my gain,
My smile beneath the tyrant's frown,
In shame my glory, and my crown.

In want my plentiful supply,
        In weakness my almighty power,
In bonds my perfect liberty,
        My light in Satan's darkest hour,
In grief my joy unspeakable,
My life in death, my heaven in hell.
                    (HSP [1749], vol. 1, pp. 245–46.)

Reflect

"Thou hidden source of calm repose" may be one of Charles Wesley's most well-crafted hymns. Some of the individual lines are worthy of sustained reflection in and of themselves. For example, just consider several from the third stanza. The word pictures that he paints stimulate both thought and wonder. "Jesu, my all in all thou art." "The med'cine of my broken heart," echoing the more intimate translation of Psalm 147:3 in the *Book of Common Prayer* (p. 804). "My smile beneath the tyrant's frown." Wesley explores some of life's most haunting paradoxes. Rather than shrinking from them, however, he affirms how God comes to us in the tensions and polarities of life, restoring our confidence in the goodness of life and enabling us to endure.

Wesley names God in each of the successive stanzas and the first naming embraces the most profound of all paradoxes: "Thou hidden source of calm repose." When we seem to be at the end of the rope, at our wits' end, God reveals a hidden source of power—an "all-sufficient love divine" in the person of Jesus Christ. He is our help, our refuge, our security in the midst of weakness, desperation, and uncertainty. He, who was hidden but now revealed and close in the time of trial, hides us in his name, shielding us from the destructive power of sin, grief, and shame in our lives. Because of this, God's name is also "salvation," the literal meaning of Jesus' name. Happiness, comfort, power, peace, joy, everlasting love, pardon, holiness, and heaven accompany safety in Christ. For the Wesleys, holiness means happiness and heaven means love.

In the third and fourth stanzas, Charles surveys the enduring paradoxes connected with life entrusted to Christ with rapid, even relentless and potent four-word phrases. Jesus is our rest in toil, our ease in pain, our peace in war, our gain is loss. Whereas in stanza three, descriptive nouns stand alone to explicate the nature of the paradox of life in Christ, in stanza four, Charles adds potent modifiers that serve to expand the paradoxical imagery. He celebrates the gracious presence of the One who is:

"In want my plentiful supply,"
"In weakness my almighty power,"
"In bonds my perfect liberty."

Wesley then inverts the order of line four (just at the right moment in the sequence) to emphasize the priority of "light" over "Satan's darkest hour," before returning to the original pattern of

"In grief my joy unspeakable."

The simplicity of the final line establishes these particular polarities as the most profound of all: "My life in death, my heaven in hell."

Edward Young's *Night Thoughts* exerted a tremendous influence upon Wesley, the following lines of which echo in these concluding stanzas:

Thou, my All!
My theme! my inspiration! and my crown!
My strength in age! my rise in low estate!
My soul's ambition, pleasure, wealth—my world!
My light in darkness! and my life in death![1]

Charles Wesley had experienced these paradoxes in his own life. In Christ he had come to know the "all-sufficient Love Divine" that turns insecurity into faith, desperation into hope, and self-sufficiency into self-giving love. He trusted in the "hidden Source of calm repose" and so may we.

Pray

Hidden Source of calm repose, although we have not seen you, we love you, and even though we do not see you now, we believe in you and rejoice with an indescribable and glorious joy, for we are receiving the outcome of our faith, the salvation of our souls. Amen.

WEDNESDAY IN LENT V

Read

Come to him, a living stone, though rejected by mortals yet chosen and precious in God's sight, and like living stones, let yourselves be built into a spiritual house, to be a holy priesthood, to offer spiritual sacrifices acceptable to God through Jesus Christ. . . . But you are a chosen race, a royal priesthood, a holy nation, God's own people, in order that you may proclaim the mighty acts of him who called you out of darkness into his marvelous light. Once you were not a people, but now you are God's people; once you had not received mercy, but now you have received mercy. (1 Peter 2:4–5, 9–10)

---

1. (ll. 586–90). Edward Young published this poem in nine parts between 1742 and 1745. The full title of the poem is *The Complaint: or Night-Thoughts on Life, Death & Immortality.*

Sing
Meter: 886.886
This hymn can be sung to "Cornwall," the tune used for "We Sing of God, the Mighty Source."

> Thou God of harmony and love,
> Whose name transports the saints above,
>   And lulls the ravished spheres,
> On Thee in feeble strains I call,
> And mix my humble voice with all
>   The heavenly choristers.
>
> If well I know the tuneful art
> To captivate a human heart,
>   The glory, Lord, be thine:
> A servant of thy blessed will
> I here devote my utmost skill,
>   To sound the praise divine.
>
> Suffice for this the season past:
> I come, great God, to learn at last
>   The lesson of thy grace,
> Teach me the new, the gospel song,
> And let my hand, my heart, my tongue
>   Move only to thy praise.
>
> So shall I charm the listening throng,
> And draw the living stones along
>   By Jesus' tuneful name:
> The living stones shall dance, shall rise,
> And form a city in the skies,
>   The New Jerusalem!
>
> Jesus! The heaven of heavens he is,
> The soul of harmony and bliss!
>   And while on him we gaze,
> And while his glorious voice we hear,
> Our spirits are all eye, all ear,
>   And silence speaks his praise.

O might I die that awe to prove,
That prostrate awe which dares not move
   Before the great Three-One,
To shout by turns the bursting joy,
And all eternity employ
   In songs around the throne.
     (*Redemption Hymns*, Hymn 25.1–2, 4, 6, 9–10)

Reflect

I love to sing. All my life I have been involved in formal choirs of one form or another. I know that not all people enjoy singing as much as I do, but there is something about song that links us all with things primordial. In fact, one of the most memorable experiences of my life revolves around a choral concert in which I sang as a sophomore at Valparaiso University. We were singing one of the magnificent settings of the Mass in the university chapel. Things had gone particularly well. As we moved into the singing of the Credo—the Creed—we all felt as though the choir was singing as one voice; the harmonies were superb. As we sang the words *et incarnatus est*—and was made human—the resonant harmonies were so perfectly in tune that you could hear what are known as overtones as the sound began to fill the space. It was as if time stood still. No one wanted to move from those tones. All was whole, perfect, united, at peace.

Musical allusions fill Wesley's hymn. He provides a commentary, as it were, on sound, harmony, and the way in which God creates, inhabits, and fills all things with sound. Here is another one of those hymns that merits slow, line-by-line contemplation. God expresses love through harmony. The very sound of God's name transports the singer—elevates the soul—just as in the sacrament "we lift our hearts up to the Lord." We join our individual voices to the grand choir of God's people that sing through all time and space. Our "life song" expresses our desire for the music of God to captivate all and for all to enter into a song of praise that glorifies God. Our singing engages every aspect of our being—head, heart, and tongue. We open ourselves to the new song that God teaches as we learn the lessons of Christ's love and grace. Jesus is, in fact, "the soul of harmony and bliss!" We listen to his song and are mesmerized by the glory of the sound: "Our spirits are all eye, all ear, and silence speaks his praise." The disciple of this Singer longs to join heart, and head, and voice in an eternal song of praise to the One who sets all sound in motion.

Recently, I was at a conference on postmodernism, physics, and Christianity. One of the speakers, in particular, captured my imagination. He was talking about the false distinctions in the thinking of the "modern world," especially the division between energy (or spirit) and matter. Contemporary science, he argued, views both as one, defining matter as "resonating threads or strings of energy." When all is said and done, in other words, everything is music—waves of sound proclaiming the greatness of the One who sings everything into being. I could not help but think of the 1 Peter text and the way in which Wesley offers a lyrical paraphrase of this fascinating vision. God "draws the living stones" through the singing of "Jesus' tuneful name." The living stones—you and I—dance, rise, and form the New Jerusalem through the masterful art of the God-Who-Sings.

Pray

God-Who-Sings, when nothing existed, you sang this amazing universe into existence and filled everything with the music of your grace: Open our ears that we might hear the sounds of your love and sing our lives into harmony with your will. Amen.

THURSDAY IN LENT V

Read

O sing to the Lord a new song, for he has done marvelous things. His right hand and his holy arm have gotten him victory. The Lord has made known his victory; he has revealed his vindication in the sight of the nations. He has remembered his steadfast love and faithfulness to the house of Israel. All the ends of the earth have seen the victory of our God. Make a joyful noise to the Lord, all the earth; break forth into joyous song and sing praises. Sing praises to the Lord with the lyre, with the lyre and the sound of melody. With trumpets and the sound of the horn make a joyful noise before the King, the Lord. Let the sea roar, and all that fills it; the world and those who live in it. Let the floods clap their hands; let the hills sing together for joy at the presence of the Lord, for he is coming to judge the earth. He will judge the world with righteousness, and the peoples with equity. (Psalm 98)

Sing

Meter: 10.10.11.11

This hymn can be sung to "Hanover," the tune used for "O Worship the King."

> You heavens, rejoice
> > In Jesus' grace,
> Let earth make a noise,
> > And echo his praise!
> Our all-loving Savior
> > Hath pacified God,
> And paid for his favor
> > The price of his blood.
>
> You mountains and vales
> > In praises abound,
> You hills and you dales
> > Continue the sound,
> Break forth into singing
> > You trees of the wood,
> For Jesus' bringing
> > Lost sinners to God.
>
> Atonement he made
> > For every one,
> The debt he hath paid,
> > The work he hath done,
> Shout all the creation
> > Below and above,
> Ascribing salvation
> > To Jesus' love.
>
> His mercy hath brought
> > Salvation to all,

> Who take it unbought,
>   He frees them from thrall,
> Throughout the believer
>   His glory displays,
> And perfects for ever
>   The vessels of grace.
>   (*Redemption Hymns*, Hymn 21)

Reflect

Our readings for today continue the theme of song. They celebrate, in particular, God's grace in creation and redemption. The hymn begins with heavenly praise for the grace manifest in Jesus and concludes with the display of God's glory in the lives of God's children—the vessels of God's grace in this world. In both hymn and psalm, all creation joins in the act of praise because of the action of God on the behalf of all.

Psalm 98 is an old song that celebrates a new song! In Anglican practice related to Evening Prayer, this Psalm can be used alternately with the Magnificat (Luke 1:46–55). Both songs are actually included in the suggestions for Evening Prayer in this volume. On a basic level, therefore, the simple recitation of these words is given a place of honor almost as important as the Venite (Psalm 95) of Morning Prayer, recited daily. Ancient words breathe new life into the gathering of the faithful in prayer. In this doxological psalm, two ideas stand out: salvation and steadfast love.

The Psalm divides neatly into three sections, and the first section (verses 1–3) calls the community to praise because of what God has done. God's action provides the impetus for the new song we sing. The focus of attention remains squarely on God. Each of the opening verses of this part repeats the word for "salvation" or "victory." The new song emerges out of God's mighty acts of salvation for us. Isaac Watts based his famous Christmas hymn, "Joy to the World," on this Psalm because God's action leads the community to erupt spontaneously, like the angels, into joyful praise.

The second important concept is steadfast love (*hesed*). One of those rich Hebrew words similar to *shalom*, *hesed* can be translated as steadfast love, mercy, loving kindness, covenant love, devotion, commitment, reliability. The claim could be made with integrity that this word should not be translated. There is a certain sense in which it can only be understood when it is "in-fleshed," when it is realized in a living relationship. *Hesed* does not imply some kind of generic love for everyone; rather, it refers to a sort of love that is promised and owed, something to which one binds oneself in covenant. The Incarnation of Jesus Christ perfectly defines this term and is cause, therefore, for a new song that engages the whole creation.

Praise is fundamentally an experience of a community. The second and third sections of the Psalm imply a corporate setting for the praise of God in this new song, and that community extends, as it were, in ever-widening circles until it embraces the whole created order.

Praise celebrates human impossibilities that become God's possibilities. Walter Brueggemann would certainly include this Psalm among those he describes as "songs of impossibility." A new song bursts forth because God is the One who turns the world of the proud upside down, subordinates the powerful, elevates the lowly, feeds the hungry, and sends the rich away empty. Perhaps this is why Psalm 98 and the Magnificat can be used interchangeably. We praise God because God reverses the way things are in this world.

Praise, as theologian Marva Dawn might say, is a royal waste of time, and that is why we do it, with all creation joining together in raucous praise.

Pray

God of impossibilities, because of your *hesed* you have saved us through mighty acts that turn the world upside down: Inspire us to join the whole creation in a new song of praise for all you have done to give us life. Amen.

FRIDAY IN LENT V

Read

I will extol you, my God and King, and bless your name forever and ever. Every day I will bless you, and praise your name forever and ever. Great is the Lord, and greatly to be praised; his greatness is unsearchable. One generation shall laud your works to another, and shall declare your mighty acts. On the

glorious splendor of your majesty, and on your wondrous
works, I will meditate. The might of your awesome deeds shall
be proclaimed, and I will declare your greatness. They shall
celebrate the fame of your abundant goodness, and shall sing
aloud of your righteousness. The Lord is gracious and merciful, slow to anger and abounding in steadfast love. The Lord
is good to all, and his compassion is over all that he has made.
(Psalm 145:1–9)

Sing

Meter: 77.77D

This hymn can be sung to "Aberystwyth," the tune used for "Jesus,
Lover of My Soul."

> Praise the Lord, you blessed ones,
>> Praise your glorious Lord and ours,
> Principalities, and thrones,
>> Join with all the heavenly powers;
> Angels, that in strength excel,
>> Here your utmost strength employ,
> Let your ravished spirits swell
>> Filled with endless praise and joy.
>
> Worms of earth, on gods we call,
>> All now challenge you to sing,
> Sing the sovereign cause of all,
>> Praise the universal King;
> While eternal ages last
>> The transporting theme repeat,
> Shout, and gaze, and fall, and cast
>> All your crowns before his seat.
>
> There with you we trust to lie,
>> There with you to rise again,
> Nearest him that rules the sky,
>> And the foremost of his train:
> We shall lead the heavenly choir,
>> We shall give the key to you,

> Singing to our golden lyre
>   In the song forever new.
> > > *(Redemption Hymns*, Hymn 33)

Reflect

The title of this book comes from the last line of today's hymn: "the song forever new." Music has filled this week, from the song of individual thanksgiving to the heavenly chorus that echoes down through the ages to the entire creation acting out its joyful praise of God. In my very first college class on worship the professor, speaking to a group that consisted almost entirely of theology majors, said that in course work we would learn a lot about theology, and church history, and the sacred scriptures, but we would spend eternity worshiping God. Consider that amazing image. We will spend eternity praising God—rejoicing in grace.

Psalm 145 is the only song in the entire Psalter introduced specifically as a "song of praise." It bears the simple title *tehilla* (Hebrew for "song of praise"). The practice of reciting the *tehilla* three times a day developed very early among the Jews. According to ancient tradition, this practice would assure Jahweh's embrace in the age to come. It is not hard to understand how the consistent praise of God shaped the lives of God's people and has the power to do the same thing for us today. Try reciting this Psalm several times each day over the course of the next several days and see if you are not drawn into a more intimate walk with God.

Morevover, the comprehensive nature of the praise in this Psalm distinguishes it from all other songs of praise in the Bible. God is great and is greatly to be praised for every aspect of who God is and what God has done. The act of praise includes everyone and everything. The structure of the Psalm demonstrates these qualities. Only the first nine verses of the Psalm are included in today's reading, but the full twenty-one verse song forms an acrostic, with each verse beginning with the successive letters of the alphabet. We praise God from the beginning to the end. After establishing the purpose for praising God, the Psalmist extols God's mighty acts, God's compassion, and God's justice and kindness. We praise God for both God's being and God's doing. The praise begins with the solo voice of an individual, but summons all God's works and all God's saints to join the hymn that is sustained, in the end, throughout all time. All that God has created praises God throughout all time because all that God is and all that God does is worthy to be praised! This comprehensive act of praise functions as the overture to the final movement of the Psalter itself. Five songs of praise follow, all of which open and close with that singular exclamatory word, *Hallelujah* ("praise the Lord").

In Wesley's hymn, all who put their trust in God are "filled with endless praise and joy." We cannot help but "shout, and gaze, and fall" in adoration of the One who calls forth our praise. Even when time comes to its end and all join together in enraptured praise of God, the hymn upon our lips will be "the song forever new."

Pray

Great are you, O God, and greatly to be praised for all you are and all you have done, particularly in offering your grace to us through our Lord, Jesus Christ: Fill us with endless praise and joy that we might spend all eternity singing the song forever new. Amen.

SATURDAY IN LENT V

Read

Day and night without ceasing they sing, "Holy, holy, holy, the Lord God the Almighty, who was and is and is to come." And whenever the living creatures give glory and honor and thanks to the one who is seated on the throne, who lives for ever and ever, the twenty four elders fall before the one who is seated on the throne and worship the one who lives for ever and ever; they cast their crowns before the throne, singing, "You are worthy, our Lord and God, to receive glory and honor and power, for you created all things, and by your will they existed and were created." (Revelation 4:8–11)

Sing

Meter: 88.88.88

This hymn can be sung to "Woodbury," the tune used for "Come, O Thou Traveler Unknown."

Infinite God, to thee we raise
Our hearts in solemn songs of praise;
By all thy works on earth adored
We worship thee, the common Lord,
The everlasting Father own,
And bow our souls before thy throne.

Thee all the choir of angels sings,
The Lord of hosts, the King of Kings!
Cherubs proclaim thy praise aloud,
And seraphs shout the Triune God,
And holy, holy, holy, cry,
Thy glory fills both earth and sky!

God of the patriarchal race
The ancient seers record thy praise,
The goodly apostolic band
In highest joy, and glory stand,
And all the saints and prophets join
T'extol the majesty divine.

Head of the martyrs' noble host
Of thee they justly make their boast;
The church to earth's remotest bounds
Her heav'nly founder's praise resounds,
And strive with those around thy throne
To hymn the mystic Three in One.

Father of endless majesty,
All might and love they render thee,
Thy true and only Son adore
The same in dignity and power,
And God the Holy Ghost declare
The saints' eternal Comforter.

Messiah! Joy of ev'ry heart,
Thou, thou the King of Glory art!
The Father's everlasting Son!

Thee, thee we most delight to own,
For all our hopes on thee depend,
Whose glorious mercies never end.

Bent to redeem a sinful race
Thou, Lord, with unexampled grace
Into our lower world didst come,
And stoop to a poor virgin's womb,
Whom all those heavens cannot contain,
Our God appeared—a child of man!

When thou hadst rendered up thy breath,
And dying drawn the sting of death,
Thou didst from earth triumphant rise,
And ope the portal of the skies,
That all who trust in thee alone
Might follow, and partake thy throne.

Seated at God's right hand again
Thou dost in all his glory reign,
Thou dost, thy Father's image, shine
In all the attributes divine,
And thou in vengeance clad shall come
To seal our everlasting doom.

Wherefore we now for mercy pray,
O Saviour, take our sins away!
Before thou as our judge appear
In dreadful majesty severe,
Appear our Advocate with God,
And save the purchase of thy blood.

Hallow, and make thy servants meet,
And with thy saints in glory seat,
Sustain, and bless us by thy sway,
And keep to that tremendous day,
When all thy church shall chant above
The new eternal song of love.

(*Redemption Hymns*, Hymn 13.1–11)

Reflect

Throughout the course of this week we have rejoiced in God's grace, particularly through song. We conclude with reflection on one of the most significant hymns to the Trinity in Christian history— the *Te Deum*. Morning and Evening Prayer in the *Book of Common Prayer* contain canticles that are sung regularly in this pattern of devotion. All the canticles are taken directly from scripture except for the *Te Deum*. While the origins of this canticle are shrouded in mystery, some scholars attribute this majestic act of praise to the fourth century Serbian bishop, Niceta of Remesiana. If you have followed the suggestions at the end of this volume, you have been praying this hymn with each recitation of Morning Prayer.

Read and ponder each section of the canticle and Wesley's lyrical paraphrase of these great confessions of faith. Invite the Holy Trinity to surround you and fill you with love. Praise God by meditating on this amazing act of praise.

You are O God: we praise you;	Infinite God, to thee we raise
You are the Lord: we acclaim you;	Our hearts in solemn songs
You are the eternal Father:	of praise;
All creation worships you.	By all thy works on earth adored
	We worship thee, the common
	Lord,
	The everlasting Father own,
	And bow our souls before
	thy throne.
To you all angels,	Thee all the choir of
all the powers of heaven,	angels sings,
	The Lord of hosts,
	the King of Kings!
Cherubim and Seraphim,	Cherubs proclaim
sing in endless praise:	thy praise aloud,
	And seraphs shout the
	Triune God,

Holy, holy, holy Lord,
  God of power and might,
heaven and earth are
  full of your glory.

The glorious company of the
apostles praise you.

The noble fellowship of the
  prophets praise you.

The white-robed army of
  martyrs praise you.

Throughout the world the
  holy Church acclaims you;

Father, of majesty unbounded,

your true and only Son,
worthy of all worship,
and the Holy Spirit,
advocate and guide.

You, O Christ, are the
king of glory,

And holy, holy, holy, cry,

Thy glory fills both earth
  and sky!

God of the patriarchal race
The ancient seers record
  thy praise,
The goodly apostolic band
In highest joy, and glory stand,
And all the saints and
  prophets join
T'extol the majesty divine.

Head of the martyrs' noble host
Of thee they justly make
  their boast;
The church to earth's
  remotest bounds
Her heav'nly founder's
  praise resounds,
And strive with those
  around thy throne
To hymn the mystic
Three in One.

Father of endless majesty,
All might and love they
  render thee,
Thy true and only Son adore
The same in dignity and power,
And God the Holy Ghost
  declare
The saints' eternal Comforter.

Messiah! Joy of ev'ry heart,
Thou, thou the King of
  Glory art!

the eternal Son of the Father.

The Father's everlasting Son!
Thee, thee we most delight
  to own,
For all our hopes on thee
  depend,
Whose glorious mercies
  never end.

When you became man to
set us free

Bent to redeem a sinful race
Thou, Lord, with unexampled
  grace
Into our lower world didst
  come,

you did not shun the
  Virgin's womb.

And stoop to a poor
  virgin's womb,
Whom all those heavens
  cannot contain,
Our God appeared—a
  child of man!

When thou hadst rendered up
thy breath,

You overcame the sting of death

And dying drawn the
  sting of death,
Thou didst from earth
  triumphant rise,

and opened the kingdom of
heaven to all believers.

And ope the portal of the skies,
That all who trust in thee alone
Might follow, and partake
  thy throne.

You are seated at God's right
hand in glory.

Seated at God's right hand again

Thou dost in all God's
glory reign,
Thou dost, thy Father's
image, shine
In all the attributes divine,

We believe that you will come
 to be our judge.

Come then, Lord, and help
your people,

bought with the price of
 your own blood,

and bring us with your saints
to glory everlasting.

And thou in vengeance clad
 shall come
To seal our everlasting doom.

Wherefore we now for
 mercy pray,
O Savior, take our sins away!
Before thou as our judge appear
In dreadful majesty severe,
Appear our Advocate with God,
And save the purchase of
 thy blood.
Hallow, and make thy
 servants meet,
And with thy saints in
 glory seat,
Sustain, and bless us by
 thy sway,
And keep to that
 tremendous day,
When all thy church shall
 chant above
The new eternal song
 of love.

As we move now into Holy Week, let this new eternal song of love fill your soul.

Pray

You are O God: We praise you; all creation worships you. To you all angels, all the powers of heaven, Cherubim and Seraphim, sing in endless praise: Holy, holy, holy Lord, God of power and might, heaven and earth are full of your glory. Amen.

HOLY WEEK: NEVER LOVE LIKE HIS

THE SUNDAY OF THE PASSION: PALM SUNDAY

Read

When they had come near Jerusalem and had reached Bethphage, at the Mount of Olives, Jesus sent two disciples, saying to them, "Go into the village ahead of you, and immediately you will find a donkey tied, and a colt with her; untie them and bring them to me. If anyone says anything to you, just say this, 'The Lord needs them.' And he will send them immediately." This took place to fulfill what had been spoken through the prophet, saying, "Tell the daughter of Zion, Look, your king is coming to you, humble, and mounted on a donkey, and on a colt, the foal of a donkey." The disciples went and did as Jesus had directed them; they brought the donkey and the colt, and put their cloaks on them, and he sat on them. A very large crowd spread their cloaks on the road, and others cut branches from the trees and spread them on the road. The crowds that went ahead of him and that followed were shouting, "Hosanna to the Son of David! Blessed is the one who comes in the name of the Lord! Hosanna in the highest heaven!" When he entered Jerusalem, the whole city was in turmoil, asking, "Who is this?" The crowds were saying, "This is the prophet Jesus from Nazareth in Galilee."(Matthew 21:1–11)

Sing

Meter: 77.77.77

This hymn can be sung to "Ratisbon," the tune used for "Christ, Whose Glory Fills the Skies."

> O my all redeeming Lord,
> All thy kindness I record,
> Me thy kindness hath allured,
> Called, and drawn me from above,
> Sweetly am I thus assured,
> Of thy everlasting love.

But is now thy grace less free
For all sinners, than for me?
Lord, I have not learned thee so:
Good to everyone thou art,
Free as air thy mercies flow;
So I feel it in my heart.

Every soul may your grace find
For you love all humankind,
All have once thy drawings proved,
Every soul may say with me,
Me, the friend of sinners loved,
Loved from all eternity.

Sinner, how he yearned to be
Joined by grace to you and me!
He was willing, we were not,
Would not sleep beneath his wings:
Grace to all, salvation brought,
Grace to all, salvation brings.

Now, yes, even now we may
Grace receive in this our day,
All may hear th'effectual call,
He would all the world receive,
Lo! He spreads his arms for all,
All may come to him, and live.

Shout "Hosanna" to the Son,
Child of David, on his throne!
On his throne of love, and grace,
Grace, which all with us may prove,
Love to all the fallen race,
Sovereign, everlasting love!
        (*Hymns on God's Love*, Hymn 14.1–3, 10–12)

Reflect

We spent one of our most memorable Palm Sundays in Rusape in Zimbabwe. The pastor of the little church where I had been invited to preach had helped us with drought relief efforts the year before, was dearly loved by his people, and lived the way of Jesus. We had never been to this particular church before, but when we asked for directions, the neighbors simply said to go in the direction of the dust we could see in the air. The whole community was already in procession when we arrived at the church, branches of indigenous trees in hand, and the dust was from the sheer number of followers who wound their way through the village to the church. Not only a cloud of dust filled the air; the excitement was palpable. It must have been like that in Jerusalem as Jesus made his way into the Holy City.

Wesley's hymn, a selection from his collection of *Hymns on God's Everlasting Love*, makes the reasons for such celebration clear. The Son of David embodies *grace* for *all*.

Follow the procession of grace through the hymn. Wesley first asserts "free grace." This is the consistent theme of his life and often preached by his brother. In a sermon of that title, John proclaims that grace is free for all and in all. This hymn proclaims that overarching message in lyrical form. People can access this grace easily because it is rooted in God's self-giving love. Above all else, grace is relational. Jesus yearns to be "joined by grace to you and me." In a powerful turn of phrase, Wesley demonstrates how this offer of relationship has the power to reconcile and restore us now. Not only did Jesus manifest God's love in the past, he offers it freely now. Repetition emphasizes his point. "Grace to all, salvation brought, Grace to all, salvation brings." And the opening couplet of the stanza that follows underscores the urgency of the moment: "Now, yes, even now we may grace receive in this our day." Finally, Wesley celebrates the triumph of grace, enthroned in heaven, the eternal proof of God's love.

Wesley's use of the simple word "all" reflects the same movement, progression, and urgency. As in everything, he starts with God. In Jesus we encounter the "all redeeming Lord," the one characterized entirely by kindness and love. He then shifts from who God is to who we are: "all sinners." Whereas our sin is transient, Jesus is "Lord for all eternity." Having established our need and demonstrated God's character and will to save, Wesley presses the urgency of God's offer of love and call to discipleship. "All may hear." Jesus would "all receive." "Lo! He spreads his arms for all, All may come to him, and live." One of the prayers for mission in the service of Morning Prayer employs the same poignant image: "Lord Jesus Christ, you stretched out your arms of love on the hard wood of the cross that everyone might come within the reach of your saving embrace."

During this Holy Week, ponder God's offer of grace to all—God's offer of grace to you. Walk deliberately through the events of this week with Jesus and know that you may always come to him, fall into his embrace, and live.

Pray

God of grace for all, you road in triumph into the Holy City and shouts of acclamation filled the air: "Hosanna to the Son of David! Blessed is the one who comes in the name of the Lord! Hosanna in the highest heaven!" As we hear these words at each Eucharistic feast, fill us with awe at the wonder of your love. Amen.

MONDAY IN HOLY WEEK

Read

Then Jesus said to him, "Someone gave a great dinner and invited many. At the time for the dinner he sent his slave to say to those who had been invited, 'Come; for everything is ready now.' But they all alike began to make excuses. The first said to him, 'I have bought a piece of land, and I must go out and see it; please accept my regrets.' Another said, 'I have bought five yoke of oxen, and I am going to try them out; please accept my regrets.' Another said, 'I have just been married, and therefore I cannot come.' So the slave returned and reported this to his master. Then the owner of the house became angry and said to his slave, 'Go out at once into the streets and lanes of the town and bring in the poor, the crippled, the blind, and the lame.' And the slave said, 'Sir, what you ordered has been done, and there is still room.' Then the master said to the slave, 'Go out into the roads and lanes, and compel people to come in, so that my house may be filled. For I tell you, none of those who were invited will taste my dinner.'" (Luke 14:16–24)

Sing

Meter: LM

This hymn can be sung to "Rockingham," the tune used for "When I Survey the Wondrous Cross."

Come, sinners, to the gospel feast,
Let every soul be Jesu's guest,
You need not one be left behind,
For God hath bid all humankind.

Do not begin to make excuse,
Ah! Do not you his grace refuse;
Your worldly cares and pleasures leave,
And take what Jesus has to give.

Excused from coming to a feast!
Excused from being Jesu's guest!
From knowing now your sins forgiven,
From tasting here the joys of heaven!

Excused, alas! Why should you be
From health, and life, and liberty,
From entering into glorious rest,
From leaning on your Savior's breast.

Yet must I, Lord, to you complain,
The world has made your offers vain,
Too busy, or too happy they,
They will not, Lord, your call obey.

Go then, my angry Master said,
Since these on all my mercies tread,
Invite the rich and great no more,
But preach my gospel to the poor.

Tell them, their sins are all forgiven,
Tell every creature under heaven,
I died to save them from all sin,
And force the vagrants to come in.

You who believe his record true,
Shall sup with him, and he with you:
Come to the feast; be saved from sin,
For Jesus waits to take you in.
(*Redemption Hymns*, Hymn 50.1, 4, 7–10, 18, 23)

Reflect

We can only imagine that during the final week of Jesus' life, the meals he shared with his disciples and friends must have been special to him and to them. Jesus said a lot about meals throughout the course of his ministry, and he frequently communicated the core values of the gospel through the imagery of the meal. Meals often functioned as a window into the nature of God's in-breaking rule—God's reign in this world. The scene portrayed in the fourteenth chapter of Luke's Gospel concerning the great banquet elicits both laughter and profound wonder. We are mystified by the nature of the excuses that the rich and famous offer so as to be excused from God's lavish offer. The excuses are so frivolous and absurd, they must have caused peals of laughter as Jesus told this story in its original setting. The wonder, however, is the way in which God flings the doors open wide. God excludes no one. God even shows particular concern for the least of the community, demanding that both "bad and good" fill the banquet hall, according to Matthew's account. Many of them come, because in their oppression, they have nowhere else to go. They come because they are hungry and they have heard the invitation. They come because they have empty hands that God longs to fill with good things.

Charles Wesley published a lengthy, twenty-four stanza hymn based upon the parable told by Jesus in Luke 14, entitled "Come, sinners, to the gospel feast." Selected stanzas are provided for today and we will examine some of the others on Maundy Thursday. Perhaps no hymn articulates the inclusive gospel with greater passion. The opening stanza proclaims the universal reach of God's mercy and love. Jesus invites "every soul." God makes room for every precious child; no one is excluded! One question reverberates in our minds: Why would anyone refuse this lavish grace? The flourish of rhetorical questions that follows systematically reveals exactly what the rich are missing. Who in their right mind would reject a feast, a special place, forgiveness, heavenly joy, health, life, liberty, glorious rest, intimacy with Jesus? Note the resolution of the dilemma: "Preach my gospel to the poor." In the same way that Jesus takes us into his embrace through the hard wood of the cross, here also, at the table, "Jesus waits to take you in."

Living in Africa taught me the significance of meals. Beloved children of God who had no food taught me the joy of sharing a feast. The central point of Jesus' parable is joy—the joy of receiving an invitation. The main qualification for the invitation is hunger. That hunger comes in many shapes and sizes. Some hunger because they have too little, but let us not forget that some of us hunger because we have too much. The poor testify to the indignity of pervasive hunger pangs. The rich bear witness to the emptiness of being fat and satisfied on the outside and starving for all that truly satisfies on the inside. Jesus simply says, "Come, and I will fill you with joy."

Pray

Gracious Host, you extend your invitation to us to come and be filled: Help us to acknowledge our hunger for you and all that is right and good and true and to respond to your invitation to share the feast of love. Amen.

TUESDAY IN HOLY WEEK

Read

Now while Jesus was at Bethany in the house of Simon the leper, a woman came to him with an alabaster jar of very costly ointment, and she poured it on his head as he sat at the table. But when the disciples saw it, they were angry and said, "Why this waste? For this ointment could have been sold for a large sum, and the money given to the poor." But Jesus, aware of this, said to them, "Why do you trouble the woman? She has performed a good service for me. For you always have the poor with you, but you will not always have me. By pouring this ointment on my body she has prepared me for burial. Truly I tell you, wherever this good news is proclaimed in the whole world, what she has done will be told in remembrance of her." (Matthew 26:6–13)

Sing

Meter: 77.77D

This hymn can be sung to "Aberystwyth," the tune used for "Jesus, Lover of My Soul."

> Jesus justifies expense,
>> Toward himself profusely showed,
> Works of such magnificence
>> Praises as sincerely good:
> Offerings of a willing heart
>> Small or great he deigns t'approve,
> Stamps them with his own desert,
>> Loves whate'er proceeds from love.
>
> Let me thus her zeal record,
>> Thus my own for Jesus prove,
> Render to my dearest Lord
>> All I prize, and all I love,
> Him embalm with contrite tears,
>> Him perfume with humble sighs,
> Till the rising God appears,
>> Mounts, and draws me to the skies.
>> (MS Matthew, pp. 318–19;
>> *Scripture Hymns*, Matthew 26:13, p. 190)

Reflect

Strange things sometimes happen at meals. Certainly this was the case at Bethany in the home of Simon the leper one evening as Jesus sat with him at table. We don't even know how Simon reacted to all that transpired that day, but we know that the disciples erupted in anger because of what a woman did and that Jesus came to her immediate defense. All four Gospels record this story of the anointing woman, albeit in various forms. Despite their differences, all reflect the same basic event: A woman anoints Jesus. Matthew and Mark both actually declare that what the woman did will be told in memory of her wherever the gospel is proclaimed. Unfortunately, we tend to remember Peter who denied Christ and Judas who betrayed Christ, but forget the prophetic sign-act of this woman who demonstrated her faithful discipleship at a meal that night. Needless to say, there are great depths to plumb in this story.

Perhaps the most important lesson to carry away from this story is that women who had followed Jesus from Galilee to Jerusalem emerge as the true disciples of Jesus in the passion narrative. Whereas Jesus' male companions frequently demonstrated their inability to grasp the meaning of Jesus' mission, conceiving his rule in terms of kingly power and glory, the women properly understand the *missio Christi* in terms of radical service. This woman, in other words, whose name we do not even know, stands out as the paradigm for the authentic disciple of Jesus and his way. While Peter had confessed that Jesus was the anointed one, but later revealed he did not know what he had confessed, the woman's act of anointing Jesus demonstrated her proper understanding of the Messiah as One who had come in compassion to suffer and to die.

In a manuscript exposition of this story, Wesley focuses his attention on the nature and quality of the woman's act. He describes the act not only as good, but magnificent. What impresses Wesley in this woman is the depth and quality of her devotion. Her actions proceeded from love and, therefore, Jesus could do nothing but love them. She understood that our own solidarity with those who suffer, modeled after the servant ministry of Jesus in this world, emanates from love. Her service to him reflected the depth of love in her heart, not only the clarity of understanding about who he truly was in her mind. Wesley describes her act as zealous, a pattern we should emulate in our own lives as we offer all we cherish and love to the One who gave his all in willing sacrifice for us. Through contrite tears and humble sighs we continue her act of embalming and perfuming the One who died that we might live.

"Truly I tell you, wherever this good news is proclaimed in the whole world, what she has done will be told in remembrance of her." Throughout the course of this Lenten pilgrimage, we have been pondering God's offer of redemption through Christ and the call to joyful discipleship in him. Let us embrace our servant vocation in the life of the world and truly live the way of Jesus who came, not to be served, but to serve.

Pray

Self-sacrificing, Servant God, sometimes we fail to realize who you are and why you came because we are blinded by our own ambition and need to be right: Open our eyes that we might see and our ears that we might hear the call to be your servant people. Amen.

WEDNESDAY IN HOLY WEEK

Read

Jesus, knowing that the Father had given all things into his hands, and that he had come from God and was going to God, got up from the table, took off his outer robe, and tied a towel around himself. Then he poured water into a basin and began to wash the disciples' feet and to wipe them with the towel that was tied around him. He came to Simon Peter, who said to him, "Lord, are you going to wash my feet?" Jesus answered, "You do not know now what I am doing, but later you will understand." Peter said to him, "You will never wash my feet." Jesus answered, "Unless I wash you, you have no share with me." Simon Peter said to him, "Lord, not my feet only but also my hands and my head!" Jesus said to him, "One who has bathed does not need to wash, except for the feet, but is entirely clean. And you are clean, though not all of you." For he knew who was to betray him; for this reason he said, "Not all of you are clean." After he had washed their feet, had put on his robe, and had returned to the table, he said to them, "Do you know what I have done to you? You call me Teacher and Lord—and you are right, for that is what I am. So if I, your Lord and Teacher, have washed your feet, you also ought to wash one another's feet. For I have set you an example, that you also should do as I have done to you. (John 13:3–15)

Sing

Meter: CM

This hymn can be sung to "St. Peter," the tune used for "How Sweet the Name of Jesus Sounds."

Jesu, thou art my righteousness,
  For all my sins were thine:
Thy death hath bought of God my peace,
  Thy life hath made him mine.

Spotless, and just in thee I am;
  I feel my sins forgiven;
I taste salvation in thy name,
  And antedate my heaven.

Forever here my rest shall be,
  Close to thy bleeding side;
This all my hope, and all my plea,
  For *me* the Savior died!

My dying Savior, and my God,
  Fountain for guilt, and sin,
Sprinkle me ever in thy blood,
  And cleanse, and keep me clean.

Wash me, and make me thus thine own;
  Wash me, and mine thou art;
Wash me, (but not my feet alone)
  My hands, my head, my heart.

Th'atonement of thy blood apply,
  Till faith to sight improve,
Till hope shall in fruition die,
  And all my soul be love.
          (*HSP* [1740], pp. 95–96)

Reflect

Jesus provided compelling sign-acts of servant ministry for his disciples. Perhaps none continues to impress us more than his washing of the disciples' feet in the upper room, as recorded in John 13. This action, like that which we examined yesterday, took place in the context of a meal—the most important of all meals, which we will explore tomorrow. Some would even argue that Jesus' paradigmatic act of service took place during the actual liturgy of the Passover meal, transfiguring the ritual hand washing that normally would have preceded the ceremonial meal. Instead of having his hands washed by others as an act of ritual cleansing, he girded himself with a towel, poured water in a basin, and began to wash the feet of those he had called. We can only imagine how startled the disciples must have been, an indication of their befuddlement reflected in the response of Peter. Before he moves forward in his leadership of the ritual, Jesus makes it clear to the disciples that he has modeled for them what it means to be his follower.

When one of our daughters was a little girl, she was invited to participate in a Mennonite wedding. The most distinctive feature of the service came immediately following the bride and groom's exchange of vows. They washed one another's feet as the first act of their life together and then washed the feet of their in-laws as well. They set the tone of their married life on the first day of their covenant with each other. They promised to serve one another throughout the course of their lives and then acted out those commitments in a concrete and tangible way. This is what Jesus expected of his disciples. Having embraced Christ and having been called by God's grace into a life of self-giving love, they were invited by Jesus to act that out in real life situations throughout the course of their lives. Jesus called them to act out their faith in love.

Wesley employed many different images and motifs to communicate the redemptive work of Christ on our behalf. For him, atonement was a multifaceted reality in our lives. It not only entailed what Christ did for us through his death and resurrection, it also included Christ's continuing intercession for us and the work of the Spirit in our lives. Many of his hymns, like that for today, explore the breadth and depth of this mysterious, reconciling work. In "Jesu, thou art my righteousness" Charles exploits the image of Jesus' blood and its cleansing power. His central affirmation resonates with a Swahili chorus often sung at Communion in the ecumenical seminary where we served in Kenya: *Damu ya Yesu.* "Oh the blood of Jesus, it cleanses me completely." Knowing that we are clean, through and through, brings great joy.

In this regard, that one stanza of the hymn just stands out like a beacon of hope:

> Wash me, and make me thus thine own;
> Wash me, and mine thou art;
> Wash me, (but not my feet alone)
> My hands, my head, my heart.

Pray

Wash me, O God of Love, and make me your own: Take all I am and all I have, take my head and my heart, and may my hands be your own as they are put to work in the service of others for your own name's sake. Amen.

MAUNDY THURSDAY

Read

While they were eating, Jesus took a loaf of bread, and after blessing it he broke it, gave it to the disciples, and said, "Take, eat; this is my body." Then he took a cup, and after giving thanks he gave it to them, saying, "Drink from it, all of you; for this is my blood of the covenant, which is poured out for many for the forgiveness of sins. (Matthew 26:26–28)

Sing

Meter: LM

This hymn can be sung to "Rockingham," the tune used for "When I Survey the Wondrous Cross."

> Come, sinners, to the gospel feast,
> Let every soul be Jesu's guest,
> You need not one be left behind,
> For God hath bid all humankind.
>
> Sent by my Lord, on you I call,
> The invitation is to all.
> Come all the world: come, sinner, thou,
> All things in Christ are ready now.

Come then you souls, by sin oppressed,
You restless wanderers after rest,
You poor, and maimed, and halt, and blind,
In Christ a hearty welcome find.

Come, and partake the gospel feast,
Be saved from sin, in Jesus rest:
O taste the goodness of our God,
And eat his flesh, and drink his blood.

You vagrant souls, on you I call,
(O that my voice could reach you all)
You all are freely justified,
You all may live, for God hath died.

My message as from God receive
You all may come to Christ, and live:
O let his love your hearts constrain,
Nor suffer him to die in vain.

His love is mighty to compel,
His conquering love consent to feel,
Yield to his love's resistless power,
And fight against your God no more.

See him set forth before your eyes,
Behold the bleeding sacrifice!
His offered love make haste t'embrace,
And freely now be saved by grace.

This is the time, no more delay,
This is the acceptable day,
Come in, this moment, at his call,
And live for him who died for all.

(*Redemption Hymns,*
Hymn 50.1–2, 12, 14, 19–22, 24)

Reflect

Both John and Charles Wesley described the Sacrament of Holy Communion as the primary means of grace. They believed that God offers the fullness of Jesus Christ to each of us in this sign-act of love. On this Maundy Thursday, as we reflect upon the institution of this sacred meal, consider just three facets of its meaning for our lives as it relates to the past, present, and future.

First, *the Lord's Supper is a memorial of the passion of Christ.* The Sacrament is a remembrance of the sacrifice of Jesus Christ on our behalf. It helps us to "remember" in the sense of calling the events of the Upper Room to mind in such a way as to make them real for us in the present moment. Wesley's masterful use of imagery in his many hymns on the Lord's Supper brings the event of the cross to the forefront of our consciousness and into our experience here and now:

> Endless scenes of wonder rise
>> With that mysterious tree,
> Crucified before our eyes
>> Where we our Maker see:
> Jesus, Lord, what hast Thou done?
>> Publish we the death Divine,
> Stop, and gaze, and fall, and own
>> Was never love like Thine!
>
> Never love nor sorrow was
>> Like that my Jesus showed;
> See Him stretched on yonder cross,
>> And crushed beneath the load!
> Now discern the Deity,
>> Now His heavenly birth declare;
> Faith cries out, 'Tis He, 'tis He,
>> My God, that suffers there!
>> (*HLS*, 21.2–3)

The most amazing fact about the cross, of course, is that this instrument of death should become the supreme symbol of God's love.

Secondly, *the Eucharist is a celebration of the presence of the living Christ.* One of the earliest terms for the Sacrament comes from a Greek word, *eucharistia*, meaning "thanksgiving." This was the "Thanksgiving Feast" of the early Christians; a celebration of the Resurrection and the presence of the living Lord. More than anything else, joy characterized the early celebrations of this feast. Through faith we receive the inward and spiritual blessings signified in the outward signs of Jesus' body and blood. Jesus "fills" the meal and meets us with the fullness of his grace. As Wesley knew, the heights to which faith can move us are immeasurable:

> The joy is more unspeakable,
>> And yields me larger draughts of God,
> Till nature faints beneath the power,
>> And faith filled up can hold no more. (*HLS*, 54.5)

Thirdly, *Holy Communion is a pledge of the Heavenly Banquet to come.* The Wesleys helped the church of their own day to gain a new appreciation for the communion of saints. As we gather around the table, we are never alone. We are surrounded by a great cloud of witnesses, and together look forward to God's promise of the heavenly banquet when all of God's children will be reunited in one great feast of love. No one celebrated that vision like Charles Wesley:

> How glorious is the life above,
>> Which in this ordinance we *taste*;
> That fullness of celestial love,
>> That joy which shall for ever last!
>
> Sure pledge of ecstasies unknown
>> Shall this Divine communion be;
> The ray shall rise into a sun,
>> The drop shall swell into a sea. (*HLS*, 101.1, 4)

In the sacrament that we celebrate this day, God comes to us anew and we learn once again what it means to offer ourselves in praise and thanksgiving as a holy and living sacrifice, in union with Christ's offering for us, as we proclaim the mystery of faith: "Christ has died; Christ is risen; Christ will come again."

Pray

Eternal God, we give you thanks for the holy mystery in which you give yourself to us: Grant that we may go into the world in the strength of your Spirit, to give ourselves for others, in the name of Jesus Christ our Lord. Amen.

GOOD FRIDAY

Read

After mocking him, they stripped him of the purple cloak and put his own clothes on him. Then they led him out to crucify him. They compelled a passer-by, who was coming in from the country, to carry his cross; it was Simon of Cyrene, the father of Alexander and Rufus. Then they brought Jesus to the place called Golgotha [which means the place of a skull]. And they offered him wine mixed with myrrh; but he did not take it. And they crucified him, and divided his clothes among them, casting lots to decide what each should take. . . . When it was noon, darkness came over the whole land until three in the afternoon. At three o'clock Jesus cried out with a loud voice, "Eloi, Eloi, lema sabachthani?" which means, "My God, my God, why have you forsaken me?" When some of the bystanders heard it, they said, "Listen, he is calling for Elijah." And someone ran, filled a sponge with sour wine, put it on a stick, and gave it to him to drink, saying, "Wait, let us see whether Elijah will come to take him down." Then Jesus gave a loud cry and breathed his last. And the curtain of the temple was torn in two, from top to bottom. Now when the centurion, who stood facing him, saw that in this way he breathed his last, he said, "Truly this man was God's Son!" (Mark 15:20–24, 33–39)

Sing

Meter: 88.88.88

This hymn can be sung to "St. Catherine," the tune for "Faith of Our Fathers."

O love divine, what hast thou done!
    The immortal God hath died for me!
The Father's co-eternal Son
    Bore all my sins upon the tree;
Th'immortal God for me hath died!
My Lord, my love is crucified!

Behold him all you who pass by,
    The bleeding Prince of life and peace,
Come, sinners, see your Maker die,
    And say, was ever grief like his!
Come feel with me his blood applied:
My Lord, my love is crucified!

Is crucified for me and you,
    To bring us rebels near to God;
Believe, believe the record true,
    We all are bought with Jesu's blood;
Pardon for all flows from his side:
My Lord, my love is crucified.

Then let us sit beneath his cross,
    And gladly catch the healing stream,
All things for him account but loss,
    And give up all our hearts to him;
Of nothing think, or speak beside:
My Lord, my love is crucified!

                    (*HSP* [1742], pp. 26–27)

Reflect

The opening couplet of Wesley's hymn poses one of the most profound questions and one of the most profound mysteries we could ever ponder.

O love divine, what hast thou done!
The immortal God hath died for me!

We stand today in awe and wonder at the foot of the cross.

This cross drove the sharp point of pathos deeper into the human heart than it had ever gone before. The ultimate confession of the early followers of Jesus, however, was that somehow, mysteriously, God was "in it." They believed that when Jesus suffered and died on the cross, God bore the sin and suffering of the world. Christ absorbed the agony of broken hearts and twisted lives for all time. For St. Paul, this was the revelation of God's *glory*, long hidden from our eyes. As one well acquainted with suffering himself, he determined never to "boast of anything except the cross of our Lord Jesus Christ (Gal. 6:14), only to "proclaim Christ crucified" (1 Cor. 1:23), to "know nothing" except this God who absorbs our wounds into his very being (1 Cor. 2:2). In Christ, we are invited to participate in a way that faced the worst and went down into the depths of human misery and endured the cross before it rose up to proclaim the victory and glory of the Gospel of our Lord. And the victorious One says to each of us today: "If any want to become my followers, let them deny themselves and take up their cross daily and follow me. For those who want to save their life will lose it, and those who lose their life for my sake will save it" (Luke 9:23–24).

Wesley draws our attention to four aspects of the cross that continue to fill us with awe. First, he ponders the mystery of the "immortal God" who created all life and whose co-eternal Son dies on our behalf. Some contemporary versions of the hymn attempt to soften the mystery by exchanging "immortal" with "incarnate." But Wesley will not let go of this bewildering paradox. We are called to come and "see our Maker die." Secondly, he summons every person who passes through life to stop at the foot of Calvary and contemplate this scene. None can bypass the cross of Christ. Wesley puts life before us as it really is and compels us to see the depth of God's own sacrifice on our behalf. He pleads for us, not only to "see" the cross, but to "feel" it as well—to let it break our hearts, for thirdly, it is all for us. Christ dies to make it possible for us to find our way home. The cross "brings us rebels near to God," or as some versions of the hymn proclaim, brings us "back to God." Fourthly, beneath the cross we "catch the healing stream." Not only does this wondrous sight bring us home, it makes us whole. A life of self-giving love becomes the foundation and goal of our own lives, and we can proclaim but one thing: "My Lord, my Love is crucified."

Pray

Crucified God, we shrink from the mystery of the cross, but we are also drawn inexplicably by its wonder and its power: O Love divine what hast thou done? The immortal God hath died for me! Amen.

HOLY SATURDAY

Read

When evening had come, and since it was the day of Preparation, that is, the day before the Sabbath, Joseph of Arimathea, a respected member of the council, who was also himself waiting expectantly for the kingdom of God, went boldly to Pilate and asked for the body of Jesus. Then Pilate wondered if he were already dead; and summoning the centurion, he asked him whether he had been dead for some time. When he learned from the centurion that he was dead, he granted the body to Joseph. Then Joseph bought a linen cloth, and taking down the body, wrapped it in the linen cloth, and laid it in a tomb that had been hewn out of the rock. He then rolled a stone against the door of the tomb. Mary Magdalene and Mary the mother of Joses saw where the body was laid. (Mark 15:42–47)

Sing

Meter: 76.76.77.76

This hymn can be sung to "Amsterdam," the tune used for "Praise the Lord Who Reigns Above" in some hymnals.

> God of unexampled grace,
>   Redeemer of mankind,
> Matter of eternal praise
>   We in thy Passion find:
> Still our choicest strains we bring,
>   Still the joyful theme pursue,
> Thee the friend of sinners sing
>   Whose love is ever new.

Endless scenes of wonder rise
    With that mysterious tree,
Crucified before our eyes
    Where we our Maker see:
Jesus, Lord, what hast thou done!
    Publish we the death divine,
Stop, and gaze, and fall, and own
    Was never love like thine!

Never love nor sorrow was
    Like that my Jesus showed;
See him stretched on yonder cross
    And crushed beneath our load!
Now discern the deity,
    Now his heavenly birth declare!
Faith cries out 'Tis he, 'tis he,
    My God that suffers there!

O my God, he dies for me,
    I feel the mortal smart!
See him hanging on the tree—
    A sight that breaks my heart!
O that all to thee might turn!
    Sinners, you may love him too,
Look on him you pierced, and mourn
    For one who bled for you.
        (*HLS*, 21.1–3, 7)

Reflect

Simon of Arimathea placed Jesus' body in a tomb, because "He suffered under Pontius Pilate, was crucified and died." The vision of Jesus on the cross, however, was permanently seared on our memory.

In one of the most powerful hymns that Charles Wesley ever wrote, we encounter what J. Ernest Rattenbury described as "a Protestant Crucifix." The hymn is a verbal, a lyrical depiction of Christ on the cross. We have already encountered two of its stanzas in our reading for Maundy Thursday. Through the power of his words, and the Spirit that inspired them, Wesley draws us into the sights and sounds of that awe-full Friday afternoon. Contemplate the scene:

> Endless scenes of wonder rise
>> With that mysterious tree,
> Crucified before our eyes
>> Where we our Maker see:
> See him stretched on yonder cross,
>> And crushed beneath our load!
> See him hanging on the tree—
>> A sight that breaks *my* heart!
> Stop, and gaze, and fall, and own
>> Was never love like thine!

In the amazing "Fourth Servant Song" of the prophet Isaiah (52:13–53:12), excessive evil overwhelms Isaiah's figure of the servant and leaves him condemned and rejected by all. Despite the cruel abandonment he endures, the servant condemns no one and issues no complaint. Through his silence he remains free and the only one untouched by violence in his inner spirit. "By his wounds we are healed." This servant image—and its realization in the crucified Christ—reveals to us a God who attempts neither to coerce us into love nor to impose love upon us. Christ exposes himself to incomprehension at the mercy of those he seeks to love. Through the sacrifice of his life upon the cross, he frees us from the fears that paralyze us, the sin that alienates us from God and one another, and the impotence to be the loving creatures God has always intended us to be.

Today, as you continue to ponder the meaning of the cross—stop, and gaze, and fall, and own its significance for you. On one level, only images, only poetry, only song, only art suffice as we explore the simple statement, "Faith cries out, 'Tis he, 'tis he, My God, that suffers there!" Words seem totally inadequate. Thought spills over into adoration. But Wesley captures the greatest mystery of all in that critical phrase: "O my God, he dies for *me*." You have an opportunity right now, not just to read another devotional book, but to meet the God of love in the face of Jesus Christ in a simple act of prayer. Own the fact that God loves you with the kind of self-sacrificing love you see manifest in the cross of Christ. Allow the vision of Christ on the cross to "break your heart." You have come a long, long way to stand here at the foot of the cross. Invite the Holy Spirit into your broken heart, to heal and cleanse, to restore and renew; for God longs for you to be a lover throughout your life, just as Jesus has loved you.

Pray

Friend of Sinners, I know that your love is always new and when confronted with the reality of the cross I realize that there was never love like yours: Open my heart to your presence and your power that I too might love with that kind of love throughout my life. Amen.

PART TWO

Hymns and Prayers for the Octave of Easter

BREAK FORTH INTO PRAISE!

THE SUNDAY OF THE RESURRECTION

Read

Early on the first day of the week, while it was still dark, Mary Magdalene came to the tomb and saw that the stone had been removed from the tomb. So she ran and went to Simon Peter and the other disciple, the one whom Jesus loved, and said to them, "They have taken the Lord out of the tomb, and we do not know where they have laid him." Then Peter and the other disciple set out and went toward the tomb. The two were running together, but the other disciple outran Peter and reached the tomb first. He bent down to look in and saw the linen wrappings lying there, but he did not go in. Then Simon Peter came, following him, and went into the tomb. He saw the linen wrappings lying there, and the cloth that had been on Jesus' head, not lying with the linen wrappings but rolled up in a place by itself. Then the other disciple, who reached the tomb first, also went in, and he saw and believed; for as yet they did not understand the scripture, that he must rise from the dead. Then the disciples returned to their homes. (John 20:1–10)

Sing
Meter: 77.77
This hymn can be sung to "Resurrexit," the traditional tune for this hymn.

> "Christ the Lord is risen today,"
> Earth and heaven in chorus say,
> Raise your joys and triumphs high,
> Sing you heavens, and earth reply.
>
> Love's redeeming work is done,
> Fought the fight, the battle won,
> Death in vain forbids him rise:
> Christ has opened paradise!
>
> Lives again our glorious King,
> Where, O death, is now thy sting?
> Dying once he all doth save,
> Where thy victory, O grave?
>
> Soar we now, where Christ has led?
> Following our exalted head,
> Made like him, like him we rise,
> Ours the cross—the grave—the skies!
>
> Hail the Lord of earth and heaven!
> Praise to thee by both be given:
> Thee we greet triumphant now;
> Hail the resurrection thou!
>
> King of Glory, soul of bliss,
> Everlasting life is this,

Thee to know, thy power to prove,
Thus to sing, and thus to love!
        (*HSP* [1739], pp. 209–10, vv. 1–2a, 3b–5, 10–11)

Reflect

Christ is risen! He is risen indeed! Alleluia! Christians have greeted one another with those words for centuries. The central affirmation of the Christian faith is that Jesus is not dead, but alive. He has broken the power of death. Just as we have died with Christ in Baptism, so we will be raised with Christ. Alleluia!

It is almost impossible to think of Easter without "Christ the Lord is risen today." Charles Wesley published this hymn, simply entitled "Hymn for Easter Day," in his *Hymns and Sacred Poems* in 1739, along with a handful of other hymns for use during the great festivals of the Christian Year. The six stanzas here from the original eleven are those that appear most frequently in hymnals around the world. A later hymnbook editor added the "Alleluias" and wedded the words to an earlier tune in *Lyra Davidica* (1708) used with the Psalms and known by virtually all the early Methodist people.

Each stanza proclaims a central resurrection theme.

- *Christ is risen!* The entire universe sings the triumphant chorus, with earth and heaven shouting their praise back and forth in ecstatic joy.
- *Redemption is realized!* Jesus fulfilled God's purposes in the redemption of all humankind. Through Christ, the way is open for all to love God and enjoy God forever.
- *Death is defeated!* Through his death and resurrection, Jesus defeated our final enemy. No power in the universe is more powerful than love.
- *Love is lived!* Because of what Christ has done, we have the capacity to love as he has loved us. God conforms us to his image. "Made like him, like him we rise" into the heights of God's love.
- *Heaven is here!* God raises us to newness of life *now*. God pours heaven into our hearts now by the power of the Resurrection. We need not wait to experience heaven in the life to come; heaven breaks in upon us this very moment.

In the closing stanza, Wesley describes four components of eternal life with God.

- *Thee to know.* Nothing transcends the importance of knowing God. Jesus, in his high priestly prayer in John 17 actually proclaims this central truth: "And this is eternal life, that they may know you, the only true God" (3).
- *Thy power to prove.* Wesley uses a somewhat archaic expression here. We use proof in the same way he is using it in our expression, "the proof is in the pudding." We need not prove God's power to anyone, but, our lives bear witness to the power of the Resurrection.
- *Thus to sing.* "Easter Christians" sing their faith. To be raised with Christ means to sing his song; rather, to permit the Spirit to sing through our lives. Our lives are songs of praise to the God of love. Throughout all eternity, we sing God's praise. That is eternal life!
- *Thus to love.* Once love gets a hold of us, it will not let us go. Once we have experienced the Resurrection in our lives, we cannot help but commit all we are and all we have to the advance of that self-giving love. "We love because he first loved us," and when that reality really sinks in we cannot help but be "lost in wonder, love, and praise."

Pray

Almighty God, through Jesus Christ you overcame death and opened to us the gate of eternal life: Grant that we, who celebrate the day of our Lord's resurrection, may arise from the death of sin to the life of righteousness. Amen.

MONDAY IN EASTER WEEK

Read

But Mary stood weeping outside the tomb. As she wept, she bent over to look into the tomb; and she saw two angels in white, sitting where the body of Jesus had been lying, one at the head and the other at the feet. They said to her, "Woman, why are you weeping?" She said to them, "They have taken away my Lord, and I do not know where they have laid him." When she had said this, she turned around and saw Jesus standing there, but she did not know that it was Jesus. Jesus said to her, "Woman, why are you weeping? Whom are you looking for?" Supposing him to be the gardener, she said to him, "Sir, if you have carried him away, tell me where you have laid him, and I will take him away." Jesus said to her, "Mary!" She turned and said to him in Hebrew, "Rabbouni!" [which means Teacher]. Jesus said to her, "Do not hold on to me, because I have not yet ascended to the Father. But go to my brothers and say to them, 'I am ascending to my Father and your Father, to my God and your God.'" Mary Magdalene went and announced to the disciples, 'I have seen the Lord"; and she told them that he had said these things to her. (John 20:11–18)

Sing

Meter: 77.77D

This hymn can be sung to "St. George's, Windsor," the tune used for "Come, Ye Thankful People, Come."

> Happy Magdalene, to whom
> > Christ the Lord vouchsafed t'appear!
> Newly risen from the tomb,
> > Would he first be seen by her?
> Yes, to her the Master came,
> > First his welcome voice she hears:
> Jesus calls her by her name,
> > He the weeping sinner cheers.
>
> Highly favored soul! To her
> > Farther still his grace extends,
> Raises the glad messenger,
> > Sends her to his drooping friends:
> Tidings of their living Lord
> > First in her report they find:
> She must spread the gospel word,
> > Teach the teachers of mankind.

Who can now presume to fear?
        Who despair his Lord to see?
Jesus, wilt thou not appear,
        Show thyself alive to me?
Yes, my God, I dare not doubt,
        Thou shalt all my sins remove;
Thou hast cast a legion out,
        Thou wilt perfect me in love.

Surely thou hast called me now!
        Now I hear the voice divine,
At thy wounded feet I bow,
        Wounded for whose sins but mine!
I have nailed him to the tree,
        I have sent him to the grave:
But the Lord is risen for me,
        Hold of him by faith I have.

Hear, dear followers of the Lord,
        (Such he you vouchsafes to call)
O believe the gospel word,
        Christ hath died, and rose for all:
Turn you from your sins to God,
        Haste to Galilee, and see
Him, who bought thee with his blood,
        Him, who rose to live in thee.
        (*Resurrection Hymns*, Hymn 3.1a, 2a, 3–5, 7)

Reflect

Easter Sunday begins the "Octave of Easter"—an eight-day celebration of the Resurrection of Jesus, which ends on the following Sunday. Octaves developed very early in the life of the church. The eight days of Easter are of particular significance, however, because the number eight in the ancient world symbolized completion, wholeness, re-creation. This imagery grew out of the Genesis story of creation as well as other Jewish practices associated with this number. Following the Resurrection of Jesus, many early Christians viewed every Sunday as a "little Easter" because it brought them full circle to the beginning of all things anew. Every Sunday celebrated God's re-creation. Baptismal fonts are often octagonal, emphasizing the new life made possible by Jesus' death and resurrection for those who are initiated into the community of faith. During this week, therefore, the liturgy and our devotional practices invite us to meet the Risen Savior personally and to recognize the life-giving, re-creative activity of God in our lives.

Today and tomorrow we turn our attention, therefore, to two people and their personal encounters with the Risen Christ. In the Octave of Easter, Wednesday reminds us of the account of Emmaus. The second half of the eight-day period focuses on what the Resurrection means for each of us as we participate in its power, bear witness to it in our lives, and rejoice in the sovereignty of the Risen Lord.

But today, we reflect upon the amazing witness of Mary Magdalene. Wesley retells the story of Easter morning with unequaled intimacy and power. He asks the question that must have been on the minds of the male disciples, even if unspoken, who remained in hiding. "Would he first be seen by her?" Not only does Jesus reveal himself first to a woman, but he calls her by name, demonstrating the intimacy of his relationship with those he loved, even now, in his resurrected glory. Like Mary, Jesus' mother, the Magdalene is highly favored. Not only does Jesus greet her first, but he sends her on a mission. She is the first to proclaim the gospel—to "spread the gospel word"—to dare to "teach the teachers."

Wesley draws a profound implication from Jesus' personal and intimate encounter with Mary. Just as Jesus lifted her fear and grief and empowered her to proclaim the mystery of the Resurrection, the Risen Lord will "show himself alive to me!" Because he is alive, we can experience the same intimacy and power in our life with him. Not only does Jesus speak our names, like Mary's, he also sends us into the world to participate in his mission of bringing the dead to life. He calls us into new life in him through the power of the Spirit and entrusts us with the message of Jesus' death and resurrection. He calls us to be gospel-bearers, to invite all to "haste to Galilee, and see him . . . who rose to live in thee." Mary Magdalene went and announced to the disciples, "I have seen the Lord." Go, and do likewise!

Pray

Victorious Christ, through your encounter with Mary Magdalene, you demonstrated the power of your resurrection and your continued intimacy with those you love: Send us forth to proclaim your resurrection in word and deed. Amen.

TUESDAY IN EASTER WEEK

Read

Thomas (who was called the Twin), one of the twelve, was not with them when Jesus came. So the other disciples told him, "We have seen the Lord." But he said to them, "Unless I see the mark of the nails in his hands, and put my finger in the mark of the nails and my hand in his side, I will not believe." A week later his disciples were again in the house, and Thomas was with them. Although the doors were shut, Jesus came and stood among them and said, "Peace be with you." Then he said to Thomas, "Put your finger here and see my hands. Reach out your hand and put it in my side. Do not doubt but believe." Thomas answered him, "My Lord and my God!" Jesus said to him, "Have you believed because you have seen me? Blessed are those who have not seen and yet have come to believe." (John 20:24–29)

Sing

Meter: SMD

This hymn can be sung to "Diademata," the tune used for "Crown Him with Many Crowns."

Come all that seek the Lord,
Him that was crucified,
Come listen to the gospel word,
 And feel it now applied:
 To every soul confide
 The joyful news we tell,
The One who gave his life and died,
 Has conquered death and hell.

The Lord is risen indeed,
And did to us appear,
He hath been seen, our living head,
By many a Peter here:
We, who so oft denied
Our Master and our God,
Have thrust our hand into his side,
And felt the streaming blood.

Raised from the dead we are
The members with their Lord,
And boldly in his name declare
The soul-reviving word;
Salvation we proclaim
Which every soul may find,
Pardon and peace in Jesus' name,
And life for humankind.

O might they all receive
The bleeding Prince of Peace!
Sinners, the glad report believe
Of Jesus' witnesses:
He lives, who spilt his blood;
Believe our record true,
The arm, the power, the Son of God
Shall be revealed in you.

(*Resurrection Hymns*, Hymn 11)

Reflect

As many churches have done in recent years, our congregation once staged the famous Upper Room painting of Leonardo da Vinci during our Holy Week remembrances. Perhaps owing to the fact that I am ordained, I was cast in the role of "doubting Thomas." I think you get the intentional humor. In the drama, and in defense of his faithfulness, Thomas rehearses the many times he demonstrated his courage, even declaring his willingness to put his life on the line for Jesus in contrast to the other disciples. I think that all of us relate to Thomas—certainly we commiserate with his plight. We, too, long for the kind of certainty that Thomas knew he needed in the face of the realities of life. He simply could not bring himself to believe unless he actually saw. The Risen Jesus had appeared to the disciples on Easter, but Thomas was not there. Despite the impassioned arguments of his friends, he refused to believe. One week later—on the first day of re-creation after life burst forth from the tomb—Jesus reveals himself to Thomas, not only offering him peace, but an opportunity to have all his doubts swept away. He responds with a statement that has echoed down the centuries: "My Lord and my God!"

In Wesley's resurrection hymn, he does three things characteristic of his lyrical theology as a whole. First, he turns the biblical figures into "us." He develops a typology that serves to incorporate us into the biblical narrative. Secondly, he applies the meaning of the story to "us." Not only do we encounter the truth through our participation in the narrative, we are captured by it through the gift of faith. Thirdly, he appeals through "us" to all. In this instance, the message of the Resurrection—of redemption through Jesus Christ—is for all and God makes an appeal through us.

In the opening stanza, Wesley extends an invitation into this three-fold drama.

> Come all that seek the Lord,
>   Him that was crucified,
> Come listen to the gospel word,
>   And feel it now applied:

He trusts the *kerygma*—the story of Jesus' death and resurrection. He believes that there is power in this narrative of God's love. He repeats the appeal to "come." He invites the seeker to "listen to the gospel word" and not only to understand it, but to "feel" it applied. In stanza two, the Risen Lord appears to "us." All of us are Peters who have seen Christ (and denied him). All of us are Thomases who have thrust our own hands into his side (and doubted him). We stand in the solidarity of faith with all who have come before and have known the Lord. Because he has captured both our hearts and our minds, and raised us from the dead, we are bold to declare "the soul-reviving word." We bear witness to the fact that his redemptive works apply to all and that all may find pardon and peace in his name. The faithful pray, therefore, that all might receive the One who lives and offers abundant life for all. Wesley implies that others see the Risen Lord through us. God entrusts us with an awesome responsibility, with a joyful privilege, to declare, "My Lord and my God."

Pray

God of Peace and Love, like Peter we have denied you and like Thomas we have doubted you: Help us to immerse ourselves in your story of love in such a way that we might bear witness to the glory of your resurrection power. Amen.

WEDNESDAY IN EASTER WEEK

Read

Now on that same day two of them were going to a village called Emmaus, about seven miles from Jerusalem, and talking with each other about all these things that had happened. While they were talking and discussing, Jesus himself came near and went with them, but their eyes were kept from recognizing him. . . . As they came near the village to which they were going, he walked ahead as if he were going on. But they urged him strongly, saying, "Stay with us, because it is almost evening and the day is now nearly over." So he went in to stay with them. When he was at the table with them, he took bread, blessed and broke it, and gave it to them. Then their eyes were opened, and they recognized him; and he vanished from their sight. They said to each other, "Were not our hearts burning within us while he was talking to us on the road, while he was opening the scriptures to us?" That same hour they got up and returned to Jerusalem; and they found the eleven and their companions gathered together. They were saying, "The Lord has risen indeed, and he has appeared to Simon!" Then they told what had happened on the road, and how he had been made known to them in the breaking of the bread. (Luke 24:13–16, 28–35)

Sing

Meter: CM

This hymn can be sung to "Nun Danket All und Bringet Ehr," the tune used for "Spirit Divine, Attend Our Prayers."

Savior, ready you are to hear,
        (Readier than I to pray)
Answer my scarcely uttered prayer,
        And meet me on the way.

Talk with me, Lord: yourself reveal,
        While here o'er earth I rove;
Speak to my heart, and let it feel
        The kindling of your love:

With you conversing I forget
        All time, and toil, and care:
Labor is rest, and pain is sweet,
        If you, my God, are here.

Here then, my God, vouchsafe to stay,
        And make my heart rejoice;
My bounding heart shall own your sway,
        And echo to your voice.

You call for me to seek your face—
        'Tis all I wish to seek,
T'attend the whispers of your grace,
        And inward hear you speak.

Let this my every hour employ,
        To pray to God above,
Enter into my Master's joy,
        And find my heaven in love.

                    (*HSP* [1740], pp. 127–28)

Reflect

The experience of the Resurrection and the mystery of the Eucharistic Feast come together most profoundly in the story of two disciples on the road to Emmaus. Immersed in disappointment and despair, two disciples plod their way home, reflecting together on the events of the past week in Jerusalem. Jesus joins them in their journey, talks with them, and teaches them about the Word. Won over by the winsome character of this unknown pilgrim, they invite him to stop and share supper with them. In the story, it is when Jesus "breaks the bread" that the disciples' eyes are opened, and they perceive the presence of the Risen Christ. Their encounter with the resurrected Lord gives them new eyes with which to see. No longer could their eyes rest on the surface of things. They were now able to see into the invisible. They were able to see the world and other people as God sees them. They were able to see the seeds of the resurrection all around them. For them, in Christ, all things had become new.

Just as the two disciples recognized Jesus in the breaking of the bread, we can recognize his presence anew with us as well. We too can meet the Risen Christ in Word and Table. Jesus makes himself present to us as we gather around these means of grace. He bids us come, come to the Table and be filled, be transformed, become real.

> In rapturous bliss
> He bids us do this,
> The joy it imparts
> Has witnessed his gracious design in our hearts.

> With bread from above,
> With comfort and love
> Our spirit he fills,
> And all His unspeakable goodness reveals.

> All people now haste
> To the spiritual feast,
> At Jesus' word
> *Do this*, and be fed with the love of our Lord!
> (*HLS*, Hymn 92:4, 7–8)

We catch just a glimpse of the joy that comes in traveling life's road with the Risen Lord by our side in the magnificent depiction of the Emmaus event by He Qi, a contemporary Chinese Christian artist. Jesus walks with his despondent disciples, but the identity of this mysterious companion is hidden from their eyes. He wraps his large arms around them both, and their hearts burn within them. He transforms a long and lonely walk home into a sacred moment of divine encounter. Wesley talks about the way in which Jesus meets us "on the way." If we but open our hearts, we can "feel the kindling of his love." In holy moments throughout the course of this journey, I pray that you have "entered into the Master's joy and found your heaven in love." May our hearts burn within us to know Jesus more clearly, love him more dearly, and follow him more nearly. He loves us so.

Pray

Divine Companion, when we are tired, disappointed, and dejected, come alongside us in our journey and reassure us that we are not alone; as you share your Word and break the bread, open our eyes that we might see and be filled with hope. Amen.

THURSDAY IN EASTER WEEK

Read

Praise the Lord! Praise the Lord, O my soul! I will praise the Lord as long as I live; I will sing praises to my God all my life long. Do not put your trust in princes, in mortals, in whom there is no help. When their breath departs, they return to the earth; on that very day their plans perish. Happy are those whose help is the God of Jacob, whose hope is in the Lord their God, who made heaven and earth, the sea, and all that is in them; who keeps faith forever; who executes justice for the oppressed; who gives food to the hungry. The Lord sets the prisoners free; the Lord opens the eyes of the blind. The Lord lifts up those who are bowed down; the Lord loves the righteous. The Lord watches over the strangers; he upholds the orphan and the widow, but the way of the wicked he brings to ruin. The Lord will reign forever, your God, O Zion, for all generations. Praise the Lord! (Psalm 146)

Sing
Meter: 88.88.88
This hymn can be sung to "St. Petersburg," the tune used for "Before Thy Throne, O God."

Come, let us with our Lord arise,
Our Lord who made both earth and skies,
Who died to save the world he made,
And rose triumphant from the dead;
He rose, the Prince of life and peace,
And stamped the day forever his.

This is the day the Lord has made,
That all may see his power displayed,
May feel his resurrection's power,
And rise again, to fall no more,
In perfect righteousness renewed,
And filled with all the life of God.

Then let us render him his own,
With solemn prayer approach the throne,
With meekness hear the gospel word,
With thanks his dying love record,
Our joyful hearts and voices raise,
And fill his courts with songs of praise.

Honor and praise to Jesus pay
Throughout his consecrated day,
Be all in Jesu's praise employed,
Nor leave a single moment void,
With utmost care the time improve,
And only breathe his praise and love.

(*Hymns for Children* [1763], p. 61)

Reflect

Psalm 146 is the first of five "Praise the Lord" (Hallelujah) Psalms that conclude the Psalter. This hymn of praise not only engages the participant in the very act of praising God, it also instructs the singer in the "way of God." It teaches God-fearing persons how to live in such a way that their lives bring praise to God. It begins with an address to the soul and then turns immediately to an act of commitment or covenant that leads to a lifetime of praise. One of Wesley's *Hymns for Children* follows the pattern of this Psalm very closely, but also provides insight with regard to the consequences of the Resurrection in our lives.

First, Christ has "stamped the day forever his." As a consequence of the Resurrection, Christ stakes his claim on this world. He declares that every day belongs to him, and all day long he is working for good in the world. All powers, forces, and people, ultimately, will bow to him. As the early Christians sang: "at the name of Jesus every knee should bend, in heaven and on earth and under the earth, and every tongue confess that Jesus Christ is Lord, to the glory of God the Father" (Phil. 2:9-11). The Resurrection proclaims boldly, "Trust this One and no one else."

Second, we are "filled with all the life of God." Wesley claims that in Christ, we "feel his resurrection's power." God not only embraces us anew because of what Christ has done for us, God unleashes the Spirit in our lives so that we might become like Christ in every way. The Psalm gives us a clear indication of what it might mean to be filled with all the life of God. It means to promote justice for the oppressed and to feed the hungry. It means to liberate prisoners and to open the eyes of the blind. It means to lift up the lowly, to watch over strangers, and to care for orphans and widows. To be filled with all the life of God means that these kind of commitments characterize our lives.

Third, we "fill his courts with songs of praise." Wesley pictures the community of the Risen Lord at worship. Immersing ourselves in the means of grace elicits our songs of praise, and Wesley specifies the source of our praise quite clearly. Our praise emanates from a life of prayer. "With solemn prayer approach the throne." Our song arises from a consistent devotion to the word of God. "With meekness hear the gospel word." Our chorus originates from the nourishment we receive at the Table of the Lord. "With thanks his dying love record." God's resurrection power becomes real for us in all these means of grace.

Fourth, we "only breathe his praise and love." For those who have tasted and seen the power of new life in Christ, every breath manifests a spirit of gratitude, thanksgiving, and praise. As John Wesley lay on his death bed, those who surrounded him could hear him whisper repeatedly, "I'll praise; I'll praise"—the opening words of Isaac Watts's great hymn, "I'll praise my maker while I've breath, and when my soul is lost in death, praise shall employ my nobler powers." Let us truly live praise to God!

Pray

God of Resurrection Power, fill us fully with the life of Christ that we might fill your courts with songs of praise and only breathe your praise and love, to the glory of our Risen Lord. Amen.

Friday in Easter Week

Read

After this I looked, and there was a great multitude that no one could count, from every nation, from all tribes and peoples and languages, standing before the throne and before the Lamb, robed in white, with palm branches in their hands. They cried out in a loud voice, saying, "Salvation belongs to our God who is seated on the throne, and to the Lamb!" And all the angels stood around the throne and around the elders and the four living creatures, and they fell on their faces before the throne and worshipped God, singing, "Amen! Blessing and glory and wisdom and thanksgiving and honor and power and might be to our God for ever and ever! Amen." (Revelation 7:9–12)

Sing

Meter: 10 10.11 11

This hymn can be sung to "Paderborn," the traditional tune for this hymn.

Ye servants of God, your Master proclaim,
And publish abroad his wonderful name,

The name all-victorious of Jesus extol;
His kingdom is glorious, and rules over all.

God ruleth on high, almighty to save,
And still he is nigh, his presence we have;
The great congregation his triumphs shall sing,
Ascribing salvation to Jesus our King.

Salvation to God who sits on the throne!
Let all cry aloud, and honor the Son!
Our Jesus' praises the angels proclaim,
Fall down on their faces, and worship the Lamb.

Then let us adore, and give him his right,
All glory, and power, and wisdom, and might,
All honor, and blessing, with angels above,
And thanks never ceasing, and infinite love.

(*HTTP* [1744], p. 43, vv. 1, 4–6)

Reflect

The fact of the Resurrection does not erase the difficulties we sometimes experience in life. We fall into danger if we gloss over the reality of suffering and persecution in the glow of Easter. Putting on a resurrection smile while ignoring the path of compassion that leads to solidarity in suffering mitigates against genuine discipleship. The crosses we embrace as the followers of the resurrected Lord often involve adopting attitudes and values counter to the prevailing currents of the time. So we must guard against a naïveté about life that minimizes the pain and suffering that accompany our walk with Christ.

The background to the grand hymn of adoration, "Ye Servants of God," helps put all of this in a proper perspective. Wesley's text is a profound lyrical reflection on the acts of praise in heaven revealed to John from his prison cell on Patmos (Revelation 7:9–11). The impetus for the hymn, however, might be somewhat surprising. Charles first published this hymn in 1744 in a small collection entitled *Hymns for Times of Trouble and Persecution*. The direction provided at the header of the hymn simply instructed: "To be sung in a tumult." The 1740s were extremely difficult times for the early Methodists. Not only did their work among the poorest of the poor threaten to upset the religious and social order that privileged the rich, during these years in particular their opponents slandered the leaders by associating them falsely with the Pretender to the throne of England. The Methodist preachers maintained both their loyalty to the Crown and their advocacy of the poor and as a consequence were violently attacked by unruly mobs frequently led by the clergy. On several occasions, the Wesleys barely escaped death at the hand of raging mobs. All becomes transparent in the lines omitted in contemporary hymnals:

> Men, devils engage, the billows arise,
> And horribly rage, and threaten the skies;
> Their fury shall never our steadfastness shock;
> The weakest believer is built on a Rock.

In the midst of such defamation and persecution, the Wesleys and their supporters found courage in the over-ruling power of God displayed so potently in the vindication of Truth and Love in the Resurrection of Jesus. Wesley's hymn summons all believers to declare a pledge of allegiance to the God of resurrection power. This God rules over all, and despite the apparent victories of evil over love in this world, the King of kings and the Lord of lords reigns. S T Kimbrough, Jr. helps us understand the relevance of this message in our own time:

We live in an age filled with mobs and rioting, and Wesley called followers of Jesus anew to stand firm in their faith as champions of "infinite love." Amid political, economic, and social injustices, Christians around the world are beckoned to turn the cries of agony and hatred into resounding praises of God. The love of God in Jesus is so transforming that it can change discriminatory laws, rectify the exploitation of the poor by the rich, provide shelter for the homeless and food for the hungry. And on it goes. Injustices fall before God's love![2]

2. S T Kimbrough, Jr., *A Heart to Praise My God: Wesley Hymns for Today* (Nashville: Abingdon Press, 1996), 193.

Pray

We adore you, O God; through our commitment to your way, we proclaim your glory, and power, and wisdom, and might, your honor, and blessing, with angels above, and thanks never ceasing, and infinite love. Amen.

SATURDAY IN EASTER WEEK

Read

Listen, I will tell you a mystery! We will not all die, but we will all be changed, in a moment, in the twinkling of an eye, at the last trumpet. For the trumpet will sound, and the dead will be raised imperishable, and we will be changed. For this perishable body must put on imperishability, and this mortal body must put on immortality. When this perishable body puts on imperishability, and this mortal body puts on immortality, then the saying that is written will be fulfilled: Death has been swallowed up in victory. Where, O death, is your victory? Where, O death, is your sting? The sting of death is sin, and the power of sin is the law. But thanks be to God, who gives us the victory through our Lord Jesus Christ. (1 Corinthians 15:51–57)

Sing

Meter: 66.66 with Refrain

This hymn can be sung to "Gopsal," the traditional tune for this hymn.

> Rejoice, the Lord is King!
>   Your Lord and King adore,
> Mortals, give thanks, and sing,
>   And triumph evermore;
> Lift up your heart, lift up your voice,
> Rejoice, again, I say, rejoice.
>
> Jesus the Savior reigns,
>   The God of truth and love,
> When he had purged our stains,

He took his seat above:
Lift up your heart, lift up your voice,
Rejoice, again, I say, rejoice.

His kingdom cannot fail,
He rules o'er earth and heaven;
The keys of death and hell
Are to our Jesus given:
Lift up your heart, lift up your voice,
Rejoice, again, I say, rejoice.

He sits at God's right hand,
Till all his foes submit,
And bow to his command,
And fall beneath his feet.
Lift up your heart, lift up your voice,
Rejoice, again, I say, rejoice.

He all his foes shall quell,
Shall all our sins destroy,
And every bosom swell
With pure seraphic joy;
Lift up your heart, lift up your voice,
Rejoice, again, I say, rejoice.

Rejoice in glorious hope,
Jesus the judge shall come;
And take his servants up
To their eternal home:
We soon shall hear th'archangel's voice,
The trump of God shall sound, Rejoice.
(*Resurrection Hymns*, Hymn 8)

Reflect

These days following Easter prepare us for God's most transformative act in our lives, the ultimate change made possible through Christ as we move out of time and space into God's eternal presence. We anticipate the mystery of our own resurrection. God's work of re-creation culminates in what St. Paul describes in the fifteenth chapter of First Corinthians. He says quite simply that we will be changed. Christ's ultimate triumph over death is realized in the change that God will bring to our own bodies as the perishable gives way to imperishability and the mortal bows to immortality. A mystery indeed!

While this powerful statement of the Apostle Paul inspired Wesley to write this hymn, the repeated refrain of the first five stanzas reflects another Pauline theme drawn from Philippians 4:4: "Rejoice in the Lord always; again I will say, Rejoice." If our life in Christ is a song of praise, then this is the keynote! Joy marks the Christian as a child of God. Wesley does not frequently employ refrains, but in this case, he cannot help but repeat, over and over again: "Lift up your heart, lift up your voice; rejoice; again I say, rejoice." We encountered a similar refrain in the second week of Lent. In that setting, in a hymn of the same structure and meter, Wesley focused on the head, not the heart, and on the presence of Christ: "Lift up your heads, the signs appear, look up, and see your Savior near!" In this Easter setting, we lift up our hearts, as in the Eucharist, and are summoned to break forth into praise because Christ has filled us with joy!

The opening line of each successive stanza provides the reason for this disposition:

- *The Lord is King*! By his resurrection, Jesus has demonstrated his rule. He alone is worthy to receive our honor and glory and blessing.
- *The Savior reigns*! The dominion of Christ begins in our hearts—that is where God's reign first takes hold—but it extends throughout all time and space.
- *His kingdom cannot fail*! Whereas human empires and civilizations crumble and fall, the rule of God can never fail because it is founded upon love and truth.
- *Christ sits at God's right hand*! Christ already rules, but his reign is not yet fully realized. We await the time when all will submit to the authority of his love.
- *Christ all his foes shall quell*! Christ has dealt decisively with sin and evil in this world, but even more importantly he seeks to restore all things through God's grace; he thoroughly overwhelms evil but displacing it with love.

- *Jesus the judge shall come!* For those in Christ, the coming of Jesus the judge elicits a most glorious hope. As Julian of Norwich affirmed, the judgment of Jesus means that all will be well.

In the concluding refrain, Wesley reverts to the Corinthian text and brings the hymn full circle. Perhaps the strains of Handel's stunning aria from the *Messiah*, based on these same words, ring in your ears, "The trumpet shall sound, and the dead shall be raised, be raised incorruptible." May that mystery fill us all with hope.

Pray

King of kings and Lord of lords, whose dominion spreads throughout all creation, fill us with hope at the promise of the resurrection and enable us to proclaim, "Thanks be to God, who gives us the victory through our Lord Jesus Christ." Amen.

The Second Sunday of Easter

Read

Then I looked, and I heard the voice of many angels surrounding the throne and the living creatures and the elders; they numbered myriads of myriads and thousands of thousands, singing with full voice, "Worthy is the Lamb that was slaughtered to receive power and wealth and wisdom and might and honor and glory and blessing!" Then I heard every creature in heaven and on earth and under the earth and in the sea, and all that is in them, singing, "To the one seated on the throne and to the Lamb be blessing and honor and glory and might for ever and ever!" (Revelation 5:11–13)

Sing

Meter: SMD
This hymn can be sung to "Diademata," the tune for "Crown Him with Many Crowns."

> Father, in whom we live,
> In whom we are, and move,

The glory, power, and praise receive
    Of thy creating love:
      Let all the angel throng
      Give thanks to God on high,
While earth repeats the joyful song,
      And echoes to the sky.

    Incarnate deity,
      Let all the ransomed race
Render in thanks their lives to thee
      For thy redeeming grace;
      The grace to sinners showed,
      Ye heavenly choirs, proclaim,
And cry Salvation to our God,
      Salvation to the Lamb.

    Spirit of holiness,
      Let all thy saints adore
Thy sacred energy, and bless
      Thine heart-renewing power;
      Not angel tongues can tell
      Thy love's ecstatic height,
The glorious joy unspeakable,
      The beatific sight.

    Eternal Triune Lord,
      Let all the hosts above,
Let every child of God record,
      And dwell upon thy love;
      When heaven and earth are fled
      Before thy glorious face,
Sing all the saints thy love hath made,
      Thine everlasting praise.
           (*Redemption Hymns*, Hymn 34)

Reflect

Andrei Rublev's icon of the Holy Trinity is one of the most cherished treasures of the Russian Orthodox Church. One of the striking features of the icon is the way in which the artist depicts the interaction of the three figures; their unity in diversity makes this work of art unique.

Rublev strikes a masterful balance between the material and the spiritual, soul and spirit, the corporeal and the imponderable. The icon leaves the clear impression of harmonious interaction, synchronized dance, mutual interdependence—abiding in love. This love is communicated to those who meditate upon the image with compelling, even magnetic force. You are drawn into the joy and wonder and mystery of the God of love.

I would like for you to approach Wesley's hymn on the Triune God in the same way you might contemplate an icon. Certainly, this lyrical expression of devotion is a work of art no less remarkable than the icon of Rublev. It is, in fact, very much like an icon, providing a window through which to view the glory of God. Take each stanza in turn. Ponder the wonder of Father, Son, and Holy Spirit. Permit the love of God, expressed through all three Persons, to penetrate into the depths of your soul.

As we conclude our journey through Lent and the Octave of Easter with this eloquent confession of faith in the Triune God, picture yourself as one of those children of God in that great cloud of witnesses. Dwell upon the love of God. As you anticipate what it will be like to gaze into the glorious face of God, let the song of love and praise fill your heart and soul.

As a final act in this devotional journey, I invite you to pray with your brothers and sisters in Christ down through the ages.

Pray

Almighty and everlasting God, you have given to us your servants grace, by the confession of a true faith, to acknowledge the glory of the eternal Trinity, and in the power of your divine Majesty to worship the Unity: Keep us steadfast in this faith and worship, and bring us at last to see you in your one and eternal glory, O Father; who with the Son and the Holy Spirit live and reign, one God, for ever and ever. Amen.

PART THREE

Formats for Morning and Evening Prayer

SUGGESTED MORNING PRAYER FORMAT

CALL TO PRAYER

Lord, open our lips.
And our mouth shall proclaim your praise.

Glory to the Father, and to the Son, and to the Holy Spirit: as it was in the beginning, is now, and will be for ever. Amen. Alleluia.

(In Lent)
The Lord is full of compassion and mercy:
Come let us adore him.

(During the Octave of Easter)
Alleluia. The Lord is risen indeed:
Come let us adore him. Alleluia.

PSALM 95

O come, let us sing to the LORD; let us make a joyful noise to the rock of our salvation! Let us come into his presence with thanksgiving; let us make a joyful noise to him with songs of praise! For the LORD is a great God, and a great King above all gods. In his hand are the depths of the earth; the heights of the mountains are his also. The sea is his, for he made it, and the dry land, which his hands have formed. O come, let us worship and bow down, let us kneel before the LORD, our Maker! For he is our God, and we are the people of his pasture, and the sheep of his hand. O that today you would listen to his voice!

Glory to the Father, and to the Son, and to the Holy Spirit: as it was in the beginning, is now, and will be for ever. Amen. Alleluia.

SCRIPTURE READING FOR THE DAY

TIME OF REFLECTION

THE TE DEUM

> You are O God: we praise you;
> You are the Lord: we acclaim you;
> You are the eternal Father:
> All creation worships you.
> To you all angels, all the powers of heaven,
> Cherubim and Seraphim, sing in endless praise:
>> Holy, holy, holy Lord, God of power and might,
>> heaven and earth are full of your glory.
> The glorious company of the apostles praise you.
> The noble fellowship of the prophets praise you.
> The white-robed army of martyrs praise you.
> Throughout the world the holy Church acclaims you;
>> Father, of majesty unbounded,
>> your true and only Son, worthy of all worship,
>> and the Holy Spirit, advocate and guide.

You, O Christ, are the king of glory,
the eternal Son of the Father.
When you became man to set us free
you did not shun the Virgin's womb.
You overcame the sting of death
and opened the kingdom of heaven to all believers.
You are seated at God's right hand in glory.
We believe that you will come to be our judge.
> Come then, Lord, and help your people,
> bought with the price of your own blood,
> and bring us with your saints
> to glory everlasting.

THE HYMN FOR THE DAY

TIME OF REFLECTION

THE APOSTLES' CREED

I believe in God, the Father almighty,
> creator of heaven and earth.
I believe in Jesus Christ, his only Son, our Lord.
> He was conceived by the power of the Holy Spirit,
> > and born of the Virgin Mary.
> He suffered under Pontius Pilate,
> > was crucified, died, and was buried.
> He descended to the dead.
> On the third day he rose again.
> He ascended into heaven,
> > and is seated at the right hand of the Father.
> He will come again to judge the living and the dead.
I believe in the Holy Spirit,
> the holy catholic Church,
> the communion of saints,
> the forgiveness of sins,
> the resurrection of the body,
> and the life everlasting. Amen.

THE MEDITATION FOR THE DAY

TIME OF REFLECTION

PRAYER

The Lord be with you.
And also with you.

Lord, have mercy upon us.
Christ, have mercy upon us.
Lord, have mercy upon us.

THE PRAYER FOR THE DAY

THE LORD'S PRAYER (traditional version)

> **Our Father, who art in heaven,**
> > **hallowed be thy Name.**
> **Thy kingdom come,**
> **thy will be done,**
> > **on earth as it is in heaven.**
> **Give us this day our daily bread.**
> **And forgive us our trespasses,**
> **as we forgive those**
> > **who trespass against us.**
> **And lead us not into temptation,**
> > **but deliver us from evil.**
> **For thine is the kingdom,**
> > **and the power, and the glory,**
> > **for ever and ever. Amen.**

THE MORNING COLLECTS

Lord God, almighty and everlasting Father, you have brought us in safety to this new day: Preserve us with your mighty power, that we do not fall into sin, nor be overcome by adversity; and

in all we do, direct us to the fulfilling of your purpose; through Jesus Christ our Lord. Amen.

Almighty God, you have given us grace at this time with one accord to make our common supplication to you; and you have promised through your well-beloved Son that when two or three are gathered together in his Name you will be in the midst of them: Fulfill now, O Lord, our desires and petitions as may be best for us; granting us in this world knowledge of your truth, and in the age to come life everlasting. Amen.

The grace of our Lord Jesus Christ, and the love of God, and the fellowship of the Holy Spirit, be with us all evermore. Amen.

SUGGESTED EVENING PRAYER FORMAT

CALL TO PRAYER

O God, make speed to save us.
O Lord, make haste to help us.

**Glory to the Father, and to the Son, and to the Holy Spirit:
As it was in the beginning, is now, and will be for ever. Amen.
Alleluia.**

(In Lent)
The Lord is full of compassion and mercy:
Come let us adore him.

(During the Octave of Easter)
Alleluia. The Lord is risen indeed:
Come let us adore him. Alleluia.

PSALM 98

**O sing to the LORD a new song, for he has done marvelous things.
His right hand and his holy arm have gotten him victory. The
LORD has made known his victory; he has revealed his vindication in the sight of the nations. He has remembered his steadfast
love and faithfulness to the house of Israel. All the ends of the
earth have seen the victory of our God. Make a joyful noise to
the LORD, all the earth; break forth into joyous song and sing
praises. Sing praises to the LORD with the lyre, with the lyre and
the sound of melody. With trumpets and the sound of the horn
make a joyful noise before the King, the LORD. Let the sea roar,
and all that fills it; the world and those who live in it. Let the
floods clap their hands; let the hills sing together for joy at the
presence of the LORD, for he is coming to judge the earth. He will
judge the world with righteousness, and the peoples with equity.**

Glory to the Father, and to the Son, and to the Holy Spirit:
As it was in the beginning, is now, and will be for ever. Amen.
Alleluia.

SCRIPTURE READING FOR THE DAY

TIME OF REFLECTION

THE MAGNIFICAT

> My soul magnifies the Lord,
>> and my spirit rejoices in God my Savior,
>> for he has looked with favor
>> on the lowliness of his servant.
> Surely, from now on all generations will call me blessed;
>> for the Mighty One has done great things for me,
>> and holy is his name.
>> His mercy is for those who fear him
>> from generation to generation.
> He has shown strength with his arm;
>> he has scattered the proud in the thoughts of their
>> hearts.
> He has brought down the powerful from their thrones,
>> and lifted up the lowly;
>> he has filled the hungry with good things,
>> and sent the rich away empty.
> He has helped his servant Israel,
>> in remembrance of his mercy,
>> according to the promise he made to our ancestors,
>> to Abraham and to his descendants forever.

THE HYMN FOR THE DAY

TIME OF REFLECTION

THE APOSTLES' CREED

> I believe in God, the Father almighty,
>> creator of heaven and earth.

I believe in Jesus Christ, his only Son, our Lord.
   He was conceived by the power of the Holy Spirit,
      and born of the Virgin Mary.
   He suffered under Pontius Pilate,
      was crucified, died, and was buried.
   He descended to the dead.
   On the third day he rose again.
   He ascended into heaven,
      and is seated at the right hand of the Father.
   He will come again to judge the living and the dead.
I believe in the Holy Spirit,
   the holy catholic Church,
   the communion of saints,
   the forgiveness of sins,
   the resurrection of the body,
   and the life everlasting. Amen.

THE SONG OF SIMEON (*Nunc dimittis*)

Lord, you now have set your servant free
   to go in peace as you have promised;
For these eyes of mine have seen the Savior,
   whom you have prepared for all the world to see:
A Light to enlighten the nations,
   and the glory of your people Israel.

Glory to the Father, and to the Son, and to the Holy Spirit:
As it was in the beginning, is now, and will be for ever.
Amen. Alleluia.

THE MEDITATION FOR THE DAY

TIME OF REFLECTION

PRAYER

The Lord be with you.
And also with you.

Lord, have mercy upon us.
Christ, have mercy upon us.
Lord, have mercy upon us.

THE PRAYER FOR THE DAY

THE LORD'S PRAYER (traditional version)

Our Father, who art in heaven,
hallowed be thy Name.
Thy kingdom come,
thy will be done,
on earth as it is in heaven.
Give us this day our daily bread.
And forgive us our trespasses,
as we forgive those
who trespass against us.
And lead us not into temptation,
but deliver us from evil.
For thine is the kingdom,
and the power, and the glory,
for ever and ever. Amen.

THE EVENING COLLECTS (traditional versions)

Most holy God, the source of all good desire, all right judgments, and all just works: Give to us, your servants, that peace which the world cannot give, so that our minds may be fixed on the doing of your will, and that we, being delivered from the fear of our enemies, may live in peace and quietness; through the mercies of Christ Jesus our Savior. Amen.

Almighty God, you have given us grace at this time with one accord to make our common supplication to you; and you have promised through your well-beloved Son that when two or three are gathered together in his Name you will be in the midst of them: Fulfill now, O Lord, our desires and petitions as

may be best for us; granting us in this world knowledge of your truth, and in the age to come life everlasting. Amen.

The grace of our Lord Jesus Christ, and the love of God, and the fellowship of the Holy Spirit, be with us all evermore. Amen.

Hymn Sources

Short Titles and Abbreviations for
Poetry/Hymn Publications by John
and/or Charles Wesley

Family Hymns	*Hymns for the Use of Families* (Bristol, Pine, 1767)
HLS	*Hymns on the Lord's Supper* (Bristol, Farley, 1745)
HSP (1739)	*Hymns and Sacred Poems* (London, Strahan, 1739)
HSP (1740)	*Hymns and Sacred Poems* (London, Strahan, 1740)
HSP (1742)	*Hymns and Sacred Poems* (Bristol, Farley, 1742)
HSP (1749)	*Hymns and Sacred Poems,* 2 vols. (Bristol, Farley, 1749)
HTTP (1744)	*Hymns for Time of Trouble and Persecution* (London, Strahan, 1744)
Hymns for Children (1763)	*Hymns for Children* (Bristol, Farley, 1763)

Hymns on God's Love	*Hymns on God's Everlasting Love* (Bristol, Farley, 1741)
MS Matthew	Manuscript Hymns on the Gospel of Matthew, Methodist Archives of the John Rylands Library of the University of Manchester, England
Redemption Hymns	*Hymns for those that seek, and those that have Redemption in the Blood of Jesus Christ* (London: Strahan, 1747)
Resurrection Hymns	*Hymns for Our Lord's Resurrection* (London, Strahan, 1746)
Scripture Hymns	*Short Hymns on Select Passages of the Holy Scriptures*, 2 vols. (Bristol, Farley, 1762)

Scripture Sources Cited

Exodus 15:1–5, 10–13, 21	Fourth Sunday in Lent
Psalm 14	Wednesday in Lent 1
Psalm 18:1–3, 16–19, 46–49	Monday in Lent 4
Psalm 22:1–5	Third Sunday in Lent
Psalm 24:4–10	Monday in Lent 2
Psalm 25:1, 4–7, 16–18	Saturday in Lent 1
Psalm 34:1–8	Tuesday in Lent 4
Psalm 51:1–11, 15–17	Monday in Lent 1
Psalm 98	Thursday in Lent 5
Psalm 130:1–6	First Sunday in Lent
Psalm 145:1–9	Friday in Lent 5
Psalm 146	Thursday in Easter Week
Song of Songs 2:8–13	Friday in Lent 2
Isaiah 12	Fifth Sunday in Lent
Jeremiah 31:31–33	Monday in Lent 5
Ezekiel 36:25–28	Tuesday in Lent 1
Matthew 1:1–6	Ash Wednesday
Matthew 6:16–21	Thursday

Matthew 11:28–30	Thursday in Lent 1
Matthew 13:44–46	Monday in Lent 3
Matthew 20:29–34	Tuesday in Lent 3
Matthew 21:1–11	Palm Sunday
Matthew 26:6–13	Tuesday in Holy Week
Matthew 26:26–28	Maundy Thursday
Mark 2:13–17	Second Sunday in Lent
Mark 15:20–24, 33–39	Good Friday
Mark 15:42–47	Holy Saturday
Luke 14:16–24	Monday in Holy Week
Luke 24:13–15, 28–35	Wednesday in Easter Week
John 13:3–15	Wednesday in Holy Week
John 14:5–11	Friday in Lent 1
John 20:1–10	Sunday of the Resurrection
John 20:11–18	Monday in Easter Week
John 20:24–29	Tuesday in Easter Week
Acts 16:11–31	Wednesday in Lent 4
Romans 8:12–17	Saturday in Lent 3
1 Corinthians 15:51–57	Saturday in Easter Week
2 Corinthians 3:17–18	Thursday in Lent 4
2 Corinthians 5:14–21	Friday in Lent 3
Ephesians 2:8–10	Thursday in Lent 3
Ephesians 3:16–21	Saturday in Lent 4
Ephesians 4:1–7, 11–13	Saturday
Philippians 2:5–11	Saturday in Lent 2
Philippians 3:12–14, 17–21	Friday

Hymn Tune and Meter Index

CPSIA information can be obtained
at www.ICGtesting.com
Printed in the USA
FSOW01n2122150217
30895FS

9 780819 223739